T0360649

The Ethics of Economic Responsibility

The Ethics of Economic Responsibility raises fundamental ethical questions related to the conceptualization of economic responsibility, that is: the imperative to fulfil certain economic obligations. It builds on a basic characterization of the question of ethics in order to introduce responsibility as a constitutive element for a new determination of economic knowledge.

Drawing on the metaphysical tradition of philosophy, the book explores the distinction between "operability-based-responsibility" and "end-in-itself-based responsibility" and also considers what is tentatively called "being-related responsibility". By presenting these arguments about the notion of economic responsibility, the book contributes to the growing calls for ethical questions to not be merely complementary to the ongoing discourse of economic sciences, but rather to sit at its core, in such a way as to restore the intrinsic ethical dimension of economics itself.

The book marks a significant contribution to the literature on the philosophy of economics, applied ethics more broadly, and the critical discourse concerning mainstream economics.

Ralf Lüfter is Assistant Professor of Moral Philosophy at the Free University of Bozen-Bolzano. He holds a PhD in Philosophy from the University of Innsbruck. Major areas of interest are Ethics, Philosophy of Science, Philosophy of Economics, and Poetical Sources of Economic Knowledge. His research focuses on the fundamental structures of sense that inform key concepts of economics.

Economics and Humanities

Series Editor: Sebastian Berger, University of the West of England (UWE Bristol), UK.

The *Economics and Humanities* series presents the economic wisdom of the humanities and arts. Its volumes gather the economic senses sheltered and revealed by some of the most excellent sources within philosophy, poetry, art, and story-telling. By re-rooting economics in its original domain these contributions allow economic phenomena and their meanings to come into the open more fully; indeed, they allow to ask anew the question "What is economics?". Economic truth is thus shown to arise from the Human rather than the Market.

Readers will gain a foundational understanding of a humanities-based economics and find their economic sensibility enriched. They should turn to this series if they are interested in questions such as: What are the economic consequences of rooting economic Truth in the Human? What is the purpose of a humanities-based economics? What is the proper meaning of the "oikos", and how does it arise? What are the true meanings of wealth and poverty, gain and loss, capital and productivity? In what sense is economic reasoning with words more fundamental than reasoning with numbers? What is the dimension and measure of human dwelling in the material world?

These volumes address themselves to all those who are interested in sources and foundations for economic wisdom. Students and academics who are fundamentally dissatisfied with the state of economics and worried that its crisis undermines society will find this series of interest.

The Ethics of Economic Responsibility
Ralf Lüfter

The Ethics of Economic Responsibility

Ralf Lüfter

Routledge
Taylor & Francis Group

LONDON AND NEW YORK

First published 2021
by Routledge
2 Park Square, Milton Park, Abingdon, Oxon OX14 4RN

and by Routledge
52 Vanderbilt Avenue, New York, NY 10017

Routledge is an imprint of the Taylor & Francis Group, an informa business

British Library Cataloguing-in-Publication Data
A catalogue record for this book is available from the British Library

Library of Congress Cataloging-in-Publication Data
Names: Lüfter, Ralf, author.
Title: The ethics of economic responsibility / Ralf Lüfter.
Description: 1st edition. | New York City : Routledge, 2020. |
Series: Economics and humanities | Includes bibliographical references and index.
Identifiers: LCCN 2020034976 (print) | LCCN 2020034977 (ebook) | ISBN 9780367623791 (hardback) | ISBN 9781003109167 (ebook)
Subjects: LCSH: Economics—Moral and ethical aspects. | Ethics. | Responsibility.
Classification: LCC HB72 .L84 2020 (print) | LCC HB72 (ebook) | DDC 174/.4—dc23
LC record available at https://lccn.loc.gov/2020034976
LC ebook record available at https://lccn.loc.gov/2020034977

ISBN: 978-0-367-62379-1 (hbk)
ISBN: 978-1-003-10916-7 (ebk)

Typeset in Times New Roman
by codeMantra

Contents

Preliminary remarks

The present research will focus on the notion of economic responsibility. Its aim is neither to elaborate on an historical and systematic description of accepted positions nor to draw a comparison between them, but rather to elaborate on a sufficiently distinctive characterization of the ethical dimension implied—if not always explicitly worked out—in validated conceptualizations of economic responsibility. A reference to this dimension contributes to an understanding of the notion of responsibility which is not merely juxtaposed or complementary to the ongoing economic discourse but rather sits at its core in such a way as to restore the intrinsic ethical character of economics itself. Within the present research, the notion of economic responsibility will be addressed against the backdrop of the question of ethics and the interrogative that emerges through this question, which in its turn requires, each time anew, an interrogating stance. In other words, the perspective opened by the question of ethics is intended to contribute to the aforementioned discourse by introducing responsibility as an element constitutive of a new determination of economic knowledge. This determination would not be confined to the definition of economics as a modern, methodical science, but would be aware of what arguably is its intrinsic ethical trait. The latter can be defined as the likelihood[1] of economics itself to welcome and sustain *human* dwelling in a *human* "reality",[2] or, to use a poet's formula, *the human poetic dwelling on this earth*.[3] However, present-day economic science appears to be increasingly excluded from this dimension. This calls for a critical stance with regard to economics whose scope includes, on the one hand, the analysis of the assumptions of modern methodical economics and their implications, and, on the other hand, the question of the ethical dimension of economic knowledge. While that analysis refers to an already established understanding of economics, this question can be progressively substantiated only as the analysis itself is carried

out.[4] This is to say that the attempt to elaborate on a distinctive characterization of the implied ethical dimension of economic responsibility
requires an analysis that goes beyond the already established understanding of modern, methodical economics as it has developed since
the eighteenth century, namely, an analysis that enables us to question
consolidated categories of economic science and thus to readdress the
scope of economics as such. In this context, responsibility offers an ex-
emplary notion to introduce a question that brings the ethical dimension of economics to light, namely, the question of ethics.

Within the occidental[5] tradition of thinking, the question of ethics
is born out of that sense of being which requires to be sustained in
and through the being of man, in view of the foundation of his abode,
to wit his ἦθος (Liddell, Scott 1996, 766). Ethics, in turn, originates
as knowledge of "the dwelling of the human being, [as knowledge of]
his abode in the midst of beings in the whole" (Heidegger 1994, 214),[6]
while man is considered to be, in and of himself, "pure relatedness to
being".[7] Ethics—in the meaning of ἐπιστήμη ἠθική—on the one hand,
builds on an understanding of being which man always already has,[8]
and, on the other hand, responds to the claiming need to assume the
understanding of being explicitly in order to become a well-founded
human knowledge. This is also true for logics—in the meaning of
ἐπιστήμη λογική—and physics—in the meaning of ἐπιστήμη φυσική—
whereas the initial unity of these three ways to understand being, constitutive of the subsequent division into various disciplines of study,
is disrupted in the moment in which the sense of being is assumed in
metaphysical terms as the beingness of beings (cf. Heidegger 2007).[9]
Briefly speaking, being is no longer considered as such, but assumed as
the reason on the ground of which beings are what they are, that is, as
the reason on the ground of which beings appear to be representations
of their beingness. Herein, the understanding of being is fundamentally transformed, as is the question of ethics. In the context of this
book, we do not have the opportunity to pursue the individual steps of
this transformation. Nevertheless, it will be shown that the character
by which modern metaphysical thinking assumes being and thus understands the question of being consists in the fact that, starting from
man's abode, the latter is now represented in its abidingness by posit-
ing "being" not in terms of "what is" but in terms of "what ought to
be". Man's relatedness to being is then based on the assumption of an
obligation: namely, the obligation to actualize the relatedness to being
in order to find a site for man's dwelling. As a consequence, man's
relatedness to being is traced back to imperatives of action, so that,
consequently, the guiding question of modern metaphysical ethics

reads, "What ought I to do?" (Kant, KrV, A 804–805). Here emerges a reference to current conceptualizations of the notion of responsibility, in the context of which responsibility is supposed to mean "capability to fulfill an obligation" (cf. Oxford English Dictionary). This is to say that current concepts of responsibility are almost exclusively based on notions of obligation.

Within the occidental tradition of thinking, the perspective opened by the question of ethics allows for the distinction between operative and ontological concepts of economic responsibility. This distinction implies that, in this tradition, on the one hand, the conceptualization of economic responsibility follows the demand for concepts that are apt for achieving specific effects in the functional contexts to which they are applied and within which they could be used as problem-solving and problem-preventing means; on the other hand, the conceptualization of economic responsibility follows man's understanding of being and thus the demand for concepts that respond to the claiming need to "say being" (i.e. in literal terms: ontological concepts) in the sense of what "ought to be". In light of this fundamental distinction, the modern metaphysical understanding of the question of ethics leads to the introduction of two concepts of responsibility: operability-based responsibility and end-in-itself-based responsibility. Here, to be more succinct, we might say simply: both presuppose an obligation that determines the ends of human actions, which ought to be actualized in the first place. In addition, this perspective offers an outlook on a kind of responsibility which is yet to be grounded in thinking, and which will tentatively be indicated as being-related responsibility. The latter is conceived in light of the already mentioned understanding of being, namely, as a response to being itself, while being, in turn, is not assumed simply in terms of an obligation.

The present research is based on selected text-passages of the tradition of ethics, as well as on the contributions of authors which, to this day, are topical reference points for scholars interested in economic responsibility. It pursues and deepens ideas that have been elaborated in recent years and that have been presented in two earlier studies of mine: *La perfezione tra passato e futuro. Per una diagnosi etica della responsabilità sociale* (2018, together with Ivo De Gennaro) and *Ethical Implications of Economic Responsibility* (2019).

* * *

The publication of the book has been financially supported by the *Free University of Bozen-Bolzano* and facilitated by the Fellow in Residence

Program of the *Bogliasco Foundation, New York*. Bridget Pupillo revised the text with great accuracy. I am deeply grateful to her. The work has been lightened by the discerning hand of friends.

Notes

1 "Today the most common meaning of likelihood is probability [...]; in this meaning, the word is also used in the science of statistics. However, this is only *one* meaning, and more specifically one that applies to contingency. On the other hand, in our use of the term, likelihood is a word of being: it indicates what is likely, where 'likely' means: apt, fair, (and therefore) expectable, acceptable, credible, promising, thinkable, true[...][L]ikelihood—and this is the decisive trait—*is unaffected by contingency*; that is, by mere (or 'brute') facts. On the other hand, probability and possibility *are* affected by contingency, for they are themselves measures of contingency" (De Gennaro 2019, 143 f.). In light of this elucidation, the words "likely" and "likelihood" can, for example, be adopted as translations of *möglich* and *Möglichkeit* in the Kantian sense. (See also the note on "contingency", p. 27).
2 The Greek word ἦθος indicates the abode of men (cf. Liddell, Scott 1996, 766) in the sense of the original dimension which allows for and welcomes human dwelling. The form of knowledge, referred to as "ethics", bears this sense, even though today's common, application-oriented concepts of ethics are ignorant of it. They are ignorant of this sense, not in that they are incompetent with regard to it or uninformed about it, but in that they neglect it in order to be applicable in the best possible way to a functional context, in which the notion of "best possible" is informed by what is recognized as suitable to fulfill the purpose of functionality enhancement. However, in this context, the question of the intended sense appears to be dispensable, if not disturbing. (See also p. 12 f.)
3 This formula brings to mind two verses of Friedrich Hölderlin: "Voll Verdienst doch dichterisch wohnet | Der Mensch auf dieser Erde". "Full of acquirements, but poetically, man | Dwells on this earth" (trans. by Michael Hamburger: Hölderlin 1966, 601).
4 In this regard, reference should be made to the book series *Elementa Œconomica*. The volumes of this series gather sources and studies from philosophy and poetry, art and science, which contribute in different ways to a new determination of economic knowledge—namely, a knowledge that does not align itself with modern, methodical economics merely by providing it with an ex post epistemological foundation or an ex post functional normativity (De Gennaro [et al.] 2013 f.).
5 In this context, "occidental" does not indicate any culturally, geographically, or historically locatable form of thinking, but rather the instant of a unique human attempt to take on the task of thinking and thus to constitute its own tradition.
6 If not stated otherwise, all translations by the author.
7 Man is considered to be, in and of himself, "relatedness to being", inasmuch as he responds to the claiming need to "say being", to "show being" (cf. Parmenides DK 28 B 6: χρὴ τὸ λέγειν τε νοεῖν τ'ἐὸν ἔμμεναι. There is the

claiming need to say and think that being is [Trans. by De Gennaro 2019, 136]). Martin Heidegger refers to this trait of man when writing:

"Um den Menschen als Menschenwesen, nicht als Lebewesen zu denken, müssen wir allem zuvor darauf achten, dass der Menschen jenes Wesen ist, das west, indem es in das zeigt, was ist, in welchem Zeigen das Seiende als solches erscheint. [...] Der Mensch ist dasjenige Wesen, das ist, insofern es in das »Sein« zeigt und deshalb selber nur sein kann, insofern es ich überall schon zum Seienden verhält". (Heidegger 1997, 95) "If we are to think of man not as the living being but as the human being, we must first become aware of the circumstance, that man is the being who abides by showing what is, and that beings emerge as themselves by such showing. [...] Man is the being, who abides in that he shows being, and who can be himself only as he always everywhere relates to being".

(Trans. by Glenn Gray, adapted by the author)

8 In this context, the expression "to have" is supposed to mean "to be". So, for example, if we say about someone that he "has intelligence", that he "has tactfulness", we consider him "to be intelligent", we consider him "to be tactful". Saying that man as man "has an understanding of being" means that he "is" in and of himself such an "understanding of being". In other words, man found in and through his own being what he already is—namely, "relation to being" and therefore the likelihood to "have" always already an understanding of being. (See footnote 6).

9 An elucidation of the fundamental transformation of the sense of being which occurred "in the aftermath of the first onset of thinking, which speaks in the words of Heraclitus and Parmenides" and which marks the beginning of philosophical thinking is provided by Ivo De Gennaro (2019, 164 f.)

1 The rise of responsibility to become a key concept of our time

A brief look at recent programs of pertinent book series and conferences shows to what extent economic responsibility has become a focus of research, joining the ranks of social and political responsibility, scientific and legal responsibility, historical and environmental responsibility, and so forth.[1]

According to a validated historical reconstruction (cf. Haase 2017; Köhne 2017), the notion of economic responsibility was first introduced by John Maurice Clark (1916) in the early twentieth century, and further expounded by Milton Friedman (1970) and Archie B. Carroll (1979) in the latter half of the century. All three authors are, to this day, topical reference points for scholars interested in economic responsibility. While none of these theorists addressed ethical questions explicitly, their contributions concerning economic responsibility do provide implicit answers to these questions, which, however, are constitutive of their concepts of economic responsibility. This circumstance is essential in as far as what emerges as constitutive of the notion of economic responsibility from the outset, and hence remains fundamental to the conceptualization of responsibility, has been, in the main, introduced unquestioningly (cf. Lüfter 2019).

The same historical reconstruction asserts that responsibility was not a prominent notion in the tradition of ethics, from Heraclitus to Aristotle and Kant to German Idealism.[2] Only after the mid-nineteenth century did the concept of responsibility gain some currency in academia, while its relevance in public discourse increased in addition to its more common use in the legal and political sphere. Thus, the rise of responsibility as a key concept of ethics is attributed to profound transformation processes taking place over the last century and a half, in various areas of human practice. These transformation processes eventually resulted in what today is referred to as "the global economy" and "the information society" (cf. Bayertz 1995).

In the course of the aforementioned processes—as a consequence of the ongoing transformation—a series of problems arose in view of which the conceptualization of responsibility in its various instances— as economic, social, political, scientific, legal, historical, environmental responsibility, and so forth—appeared to be indicated. This echoes the promise that responsibility as such could serve as a suitable means to possible solutions. In other words, in the course of this transformation, and constitutive of the processes within which and as which it occurred, the growing demand for a kind of conceptualization came to the fore, through which responsibility was expected to become applicable to an increasing complexity in various areas of human practice by developing its problem-solving and problem-preventing potential in the most effective way. Among the most frequently mentioned applications are problems related to the environmental crisis, the climate crisis, the health crisis, the social crisis, the migration crisis, and the financial crisis. All of these examples are, at least in part, associated in one way or another with economics, which is considered to be a relevant factor in the development as well as the proliferation of all these crises (cf. Bayertz, Beck 2017). In addition, following the global economic crises of the past years, economic science, as it has developed since the eighteenth century, has been challenged with regard to its manner of conceiving, and, consequently, acting upon concrete phenomena. One of the main points of criticism refers to the circumstance that modern economic science builds on a process of abstraction (cf. Gedinat 2015). Within this process, beings are considered as expedients to economic rationality—simply put, as expedients to the optimization of the cost-performance ratio. However, this optimization is incapable, on its own terms, of providing any measure of sufficiency, that is, a measure that allows for ethical human practices. In fact, as will be shown at a later stage of this book, the character of sufficiency is constitutive of the traditional notion of ethics. On the other hand, the actualization of economic optimization is characterized by an intrinsic—and, therefore, in principle—unsurmountable insufficiency; as a consequence, any attained measure of provided means will necessarily be deficient. What is involved as a means in this optimization is not a being considered in its essence and existence, but a value established on the basis of the degree to which that being functions as a resource capable to effect the optimization of the cost-performance ratio.

Notes

1 To name a few examples: Alemann (2015); Aras, Growrher (2010); Balluchi, Furlotti (2017); Davila (2016); De Gennaro, Lüfter (2018); Delbeck (2008);

Haase (2017); Heidbrink (2008), Köhne (2017); Lüfter (2019); Miller (2006); Müller-Christ (2014); Nilikant (2012); Saba Bazargan-Forward, Tollefsen (2020); Velasquez (2003); Vogel (2005, 2010).

2 Following the historical reconstruction, the notion of responsibility is commonly related to terms like "τὰ ἐφ' ἡμῖν", "αἰτία", "libero arbitrio", "in nostra potestate", "meritum", "demeritum", "Schuld", "Bürgschaft", "liability", "culpability", "accountability", etc. These terms are traceable to the writings of thinkers such as Plato, Aristotle, Saint Augustine, Thomas Aquinas, Kant, and Hegel (Fonnesu 2017; Sauvè Meyer, Hause 2017). The routine of adopting these terms as synonymous precursors of "responsibility", and assuming, therefore, that they translate its meaning in an absolute or at least an approximate way, is problematic and offers an opportunity for research in its own right.

2 Two kinds of responsibility

What remains unseen within the aforementioned historical reconstruction is a means of allowing for a distinction which traces back, that is, reduces, responsibility to its ethical dimension: the distinction between an operative concept of responsibility and an ontological concept of responsibility.

2.1 The guiding question of modern ethics

2.1.1 The imperative of operability

In fact, the rise of responsibility as a key concept of ethics during the last century and a half is born out of a precise demand: formally speaking, the demand for solutions to those problems that arose in and as consequences of the aforementioned transformation processes in various areas of human practice. Accordingly, the conceptualization of responsibility was constitutively informed by what might be referred to as the imperative of operability. From the outset, the imperative of operability, which is constitutive of the demand in question, required the aptness of responsibility to achieve an effect in a functional context, that is, a context consisting exclusively of effects and their relations. This implies that any purpose is an effect in view of the attainment of a further effect, and never an end in itself. This implication resulted in an operative concept of responsibility, related to already constituted functional contexts, to which it could be applied and within which it could be effectively used as a means for the actualization of purposes having the aforementioned effect-character. In this manner, the operative concept of responsibility is the result of a precise demand and its inherent imperative of operability.

Under the premise of this demand, and subject to its inherent imperative, certain events which occurred as part of the aforementioned transformation processes appeared to be problematic, whereas others did not.[1] Still formally speaking, the problematic character of events appeared as such on the basis of this demand and its inherent imperative, or rather on the basis of the assumed (but as such never clarified) reason for this demand. Thus, the events that appeared problematic were those which deferred or prevented the actualization of that assumed reason, which, in turn, gives rise to a specific, in-itself operative, obligation that ought to be fulfilled. On the other hand, it is precisely this obligation, that is, the obligation to attain certain effects, which, within any specific functional context, offers a criterion for judging which human practices are responsible (i.e. literally "capable to fulfill that obligation"[2]) and which are not.

The decisive aspect for our considerations is that the problematic character of events is by no means an absolute given, but depends on a context which in its turn builds on the assumption of an obligation that demands to be fulfilled. Within this context, the problem-preventing and problem-solving potential of responsibility comes to the fore, while it is manifest that the operative character of responsibility is thoroughly informed by the obligation assumed within the functional context, which (that obligation), *independently of its content*, is an operative obligation, where "operative obligation" means an obligation that, in the absence of an end in itself, remains an obligation based on the circumstance that it is functional to the achievement of an effect.[3] In this way, however, the ethical character of responsibility cannot be established in a sufficiently sound way.

2.1.2 *The imperative of perfectibility*

For again, the notion of responsibility that has emerged so far is in need of a reason on the grounds of which the establishment of the determining obligation becomes likely and is justified. However, the mere assumption of such an obligation is an insufficient condition for deciding whether a particular human practice committed to the fulfillment of that obligation can be considered to be ethically responsible or not. According to the metaphysical tradition of ethics,[4] only an obligation derived from an end in itself is ethical.

In fact, within the metaphysical tradition of ethics, the establishment of an obligation that needed to be fulfilled was grounded on the idea of a "highest truth". The highest truth is true in itself and allows for the determination of an obligation which, in turn, is necessary in itself. As such, it constitutes a sufficient criterion for the distinction of what can be considered as true responsibility and what, on the other hand, cannot. Within the tradition of metaphysical ethics, only true obligations were assumed to be binding in an ethically relevant way.

According to Friedrich Nietzsche's diagnosis of that tradition, its determinant is the demand that all human life should be subordinated to the idea of a highest truth by putting it entirely under the control of the ruling power of that truth (cf. Heidegger 1998, 102).[5] What ought to be actualized in the first place is the highest truth itself, which involves the promise of a likely perfection. Thus, within this tradition, ethical imperatives are grounded on principles of perfection. These principles serve as a source of the likely accomplishment of each being. Each being, in virtue of its relation to such a principle of perfection, appears to be perfectible, and therefore (depending on its degree of perfection) true (cf. De Gennaro, Lüfter 2018, 149). Here, truth is considered to be the element on which human beings ultimately rely for the determination of the ethical character of their practices. The latter are considered to be ethical inasmuch as they are themselves an actualization of the highest truth. The truth, in turn, is what ought to be actualized.

According to Nietzsche's diagnosis of metaphysical ethics, the highest truth was considered to be that which is "not yet", or that which is "yet to be". In fact, to pose the notion of a highest truth that ought to be actualized, along with the superelevation of that highest truth into a transcendental dimension, implies a constant discrepancy between what is (the present) and what, beyond that, ought to be, but is not (the future). Nietzsche recognizes this discrepancy as constitutive of the tradition of ethics and characterizes the man who assumes the discrepancy itself as the grounds of his morality as "a slave of the future" (Heidegger 1998, 103).[6]

2.1.3 *The first formal ground of any necessity to act*

This raises the following question that is implicit in those concepts of responsibility which assume an obligation that is necessary in itself: "What is the future of responsibility?" This is not to be understood in terms of whether and to what extent concepts of responsibility will be discussed in the days to come nor in terms of whether and to what extent concepts of responsibility will be at the center of social, political, and economic debates, but rather in the sense of how responsibility itself relates to the future, and how the notion of future is affected and conditioned by the understanding of responsibility. More specifically the question is, if and in what way different concepts of responsibility can conceive of something like an open future.

The question concerning the future of responsibility is implicitly addressed in the guiding question of modern ethics formulated in a passage of Immanuel Kant's *Critique of Pure Reason*:

Alles Interesse meiner Vernunft (das spekulative sowohl, als das praktische) vereinigt sich in folgenden drei Fragen: 1. Was kann ich wissen? 2. Was soll ich tun? 3. Was darf ich hoffen?

(Kant, KrV, A 804–805)

All the interests of my reason (speculative as well as practical) combine in the following three questions: 1. What can I do? 2. What ought I to do? 3. For what may I hope?[7]

It can be noted how the second of these three questions, the so-called practical question, refers to the future and provides orientation by indicating that

[...] man soll dies oder jenes tun und das andere lassen.

(Kant, UD, AA 02: 96–97)

[...] one ought to do this or that, and abstain from doing the other.[8]

Through the "ought to", we are reached by a demand which obliges us, that is, expects us to respond to it, and to do so in a certain manner. The demand which originates from the ought claims that we expose ourselves to it and, in admitting it, agree to fulfill it as what it is, namely, an end in itself. This end is that in which true responsibility consists, according to the metaphysical tradition of ethics, and here specifically according to Kant's ethical position. As we can see, the "ought to" sets the tone for "what is to be". It sets the tone for what, in its absence, is nevertheless present, claiming fulfillment, claiming actualization. What ought to be (and is not yet) fulfilled is the source of each being's sense, and as such demands to be actualized. In this manner, that which claims to be fulfilled defines the future of any responsible human practice, while responsibility itself is defined as a (appropriate) relation to the future. In this determination of the "ought to", Kant recognizes the first formal ground of any true necessity to act, that is, of any true obligation. In a telling passage of his pre-critical writing, *Inquiry into the Distinctness of the Principles of Natural Theology and Morals*, he argues:

Man soll dieses oder jenes tun und das andre lassen; dies ist die Formel, unter welcher eine jede Verbindlichkeit ausgesprochen wird.

(Kant, UD, AA 02: A 96–97)

The formula by means of which any such obligation is expressed is this: One ought to do this or that and abstain from doing the other.[9]

And he continues with a plain, yet remarkable, distinction that brings us directly to the heart of his elucidation:

> Nun drückt jedes Sollen eine Notwendigkeit der Handlung aus und ist einer zwiefachen Bedeutung fähig. Ich soll nämlich entweder etwas tun (als ein Mittel), wenn ich etwas anders (als einen Zweck) will, oder ich soll unmittelbar etwas anders (als einen Zweck) tun und wirklich machen. Das erstere könnte man die Notwendigkeit der Mittel (necessitatem problematicam), das zweite die Notwendigkeit der Zwecke (necessitatem legalem) nennen. Die erstere Art der Notwendigkeit zeigt gar keine Verbindlichkeit an, sondern nur die Vorschrift als die Auflösung in einem Problem, welche Mittel diejenige sind, deren ich mich bedienen müsse, wie ich einen gewissen Zweck erreichen will. Wer einem andern vorschreibt, welche Handlungen er ausüben oder unterlassen müsse, wenn er seine Glückseligkeit befördern wollte, der könnte wohl zwar vielleicht alle Lehren der Moral darunter bringen, aber sie sind alsdann nicht mehr Verbindlichkeiten, sondern etwa so, wie es eine Verbindlichkeit wäre, zwei Kreuzbogen zu machen, wenn ich eine gerade Linie in zwei gleiche Teile zerfällen will, d. i. es sind gar nicht Verbindlichkeiten, sondern nur Anweisungen eines geschickten Verhaltens, wenn man einen Zweck erreichen will. Da nun der Gebrauch der Mittel keine andere Notwendigkeit hat, als diejenige, so dem Zwecke zukommt, so sind so lange alle Handlungen, die die Moral unter der Bedingung gewisser Zwecke vorschreibt, zufällig und können keine Verbindlichkeiten heißen, so lange sie nicht einem an sich notwendigen Zwecke untergeordnet werden.
>
> (Kant, UD, AA 02: A 96–97)

Now, every ought to expresses a necessity of the action is capable of two meanings. To be specific, either I ought to do something (as a means) if I want something else (as an end), or I ought immediately do something else (as an end) and realize it. The former may be called the necessity of the means (necessitas problematicam), and the latter the necessity of the ends (necessitas legalem). The first kind of necessity does not indicate any obligation at all. It merely specifies a prescription as the solution to the problem concerning the means I must employ if I am to attain a certain end. If one person tells another what action he must perform or what actions he must abstain from performing if he wishes to advance his happiness, he might perhaps be able, I suppose, to subsume all the teaching of morality under his prescriptions. They are not, however, obligations any longer except in the sense in which it would be my obligation to draw two intersecting arcs if I wanted to bisect a straight line into two equal parts. In other words, they would not be obligations at all; they would simply be recommendations to adopt a suitable procedure, if one wished to attain a given end. Now since no other necessity attaches to the employment of means than that which belongs to the end, all the actions which are prescribed by morality under the conditions of certain ends are contingent. They cannot be called obligations as long as they are not subordinated to an end necessary in itself.[10]

In the quoted passage, Kant refrains from defining more closely that in which the assumed necessity consists. He concludes, however, by stating the following proposition, which he defines as "the first formal ground of any necessity to act" that has an ethical relevance:

> [...] Unterlasse das, wodurch die durch dich größtmögliche Voll—
> kommenheit verhindert wird.
>
> (Kant, UD, AA 02: A96–97)

> [...] abstain from doing that which will hinder the realization of the greatest achievable accomplishment.[11]

Actualizing the greatest accomplishment achievable through human practices is the first formal ground of any true, ethically relevant obligation to act. In other words, true responsibility consists in the capability to fulfill the greatest accomplishment that is achievable through human practices, which then, and only then, can be considered to be ethical.

As a consequence, it can be said that, within the metaphysical tradition of ethics, the aforementioned imperative of operability has the status of a "simple recommendation". Such recommendations have the same character as that which Kant calls "hypothetical" or "conditional" imperatives. In other words, they are second-order imperatives, in that they are conditional upon first-order or categorical (absolute, unconditional) imperatives.

"Obligations" deriving from second-order imperatives are not necessary in themselves, and thus, strictly speaking, not obligations at all; rather, according to Kant's distinction between "necessities of the means" and "necessities of the ends", they are simple recommendation for suitable procedures, which one can apply as long as one wishes to attain an end that is not in itself necessary. Non-necessary ends can be defined as contingent ends. In a Kantian perspective, the concepts of responsibility derived from simple recommendations, or "second-order obligations", are not concepts of true responsibility, and thus are of no ethical relevance. In other words, in this case, the reason on the basis of which the ethical character was traditionally recognized is lacking. As a consequence, operability-based concepts of responsibility, which can only be described as responding to recommendations, are inherently insufficient in terms of metaphysical ethics (cf. De Gennaro, Lüfter 2018).

The conceptualization of responsibility informed by the imperative of operativity is at the basis of the rise of responsibility to become a key concept of contemporary ethics. In light of Kant's distinction between first-order imperatives, built on obligations necessary in themselves (i.e. "necessities of the ends"), and second-order imperatives, built on simple recommendations ("necessities of the means"), the insufficiency of that key concept, in terms of the requirements of metaphysical ethics, has been demonstrated. This circumstance implies that, in the course of the aforementioned transformation processes over the past century and a half, the understanding of ethics likewise underwent a fundamental transformation. In analogy to the insufficiency of the current operative concepts of responsibility, that understanding of ethics must also be defined as insufficient. A consequence of that fundamental transformation is the reversal of the relation between ethics and economics. This relation was traditionally defined in terms of distinct forms of knowledge: on the one hand, there was a form of knowledge engaged in the determination of the ultimate ends of human action, that is, ethics; on the other hand, there was a form of knowledge engaged in the production, allocation, and consumption of those means through which the mentioned ends could be realized, that is, economics. As result of that transformation, an understanding of economics came to the fore which put economics in the position to determine autonomously the ends of human action that ought to be actualized in the first place (cf. De Gennaro 2006, 78). On the other hand, ethics became a form of knowledge with prevalently corrective, or, in any case, ancillary functions. Thus, ethics itself turned into an operative form of knowledge, which could be applied to predefined economic purposes, by making itself available as a means for corrective actions within an already established functional context.

It can be said that the development of operative concepts of responsibility goes hand in hand with the development of problem-oriented forms of applied ethics. Hence, ethics became the label for a form of knowledge which is expected to provide a system of norms for the orientation of human practices within a predefined functional context determined by the imperative of operability. This is to say that ethics came to designate a form of knowledge which is fundamentally different from the traditional understanding of ethics. As our considerations concerning a "sufficient" understanding of ethics suggests, what could at first sight appear to be a mere distinction between different forms of ethics is, in truth, a distinction in kind. In fact, that distinction reveals a necessity which requires the rethinking of the question: "What is ethics?"

2.2 Operability-based and end-in-itself-based responsibility

Let us take a step back and consider once again the peculiar obligation on which (over the last century and half, as a consequence of profound transformation processes in various areas of human practices) the rise of responsibility as a key concept of ethics was built. This obligation was assumed as "sufficient" reason[12] of operative concepts of responsibility, with their distinctive problem-solving and problem-preventing character. However, the fact of assuming that obligation as a "sufficient" reason is by no means evident.

Indeed, that obligation must be interrogated in what it is in the first place, to wit, an assumption. As an assumption, the obligation is still open to question and not an absolute given that precludes any further questioning from the outset. What is open to question, in order to be known as such, requires the capability to respond to its openness by adopting an appropriate interrogative stance. In fact, that openness presents itself as prompting and requiring an interrogation. In other words, the openness itself originates an interrogation. Consequently, we call this openness an interrogative openness, or, simply, an interrogative. Thus, we can say that the assumption of a contingent obligation recommits to an interrogative that, on the one hand, is open to questioning and thus requires the capability to respond to it through an interrogation; on the other hand, the elusion of this interrogative (i.e. the failure to respond to it) is constitutive of what was assumed as the "sufficient" reason for the conceptualization of responsibility in operative terms. This is to say that the conceptualization of responsibility in operative terms is grounded in an original, but neglected, interrogative which as such requires the capability to respond to it. In other words, that interrogative requires an original responsibility.

As a result of the discussion of the previous chapters, two distinct kinds of responsibility have emerged thus far.[13] On the one hand, there is operability-based responsibility: in this case, the conceptualization of responsibility is related to and based on a form of obligation which is not necessary in itself and therefore sustains second-order imperatives such as the imperative of operability. In light of such imperatives, the answers given to the guiding question of modern ethics—"What ought I to do?"—have the character of conditional obligations, that is, simple recommendations. On the other hand, there is end-in-itself-based responsibility: in this case, the conceptualization of responsibility is related to and based on a form of obligation which is necessary in itself and therefore sustains first-order imperatives, such as the Kantian categorical imperative. In light of such imperatives, the answers given to the guiding question of ethics—"What ought I to do?"—have the character of unconditional obligations.

However, as already anticipated (see p. IX), a third kind of responsibility can be conceived, namely, one which emerges in light of the response to being itself, where the latter is, in turn, not conceived offhand as an obligation—neither in the sense of an operative obligation[14] nor in the sense of an obligation necessary in itself[15]—but as containing within itself the need for a human response, that is, the need of being sustained in and through the being of man. This third kind of responsibility, which does not give rise to an obligation, will be introduced tentatively as "being-related responsibility". In order to see the necessity of its introduction, we must characterize more rigorously the two levels of conceptualization that have been distinguished so far, as well as their relation.

2.3 Operative concepts and ontological concepts of responsibility

In general, we can distinguish, on the one hand, operative concepts, such as the operative concept of responsibility, which respond to an operative obligation and are therefore subject to a conditional imperative. On the other hand, there are concepts, which respond to an obligation that is necessary in itself, and therefore subject to an unconditional imperative. We call the latter "ontological concepts" inasmuch as they are assumed as responses to a precise interrogative which, on the other hand, is neglected (i.e. ignored) by merely operative concepts, namely, the interrogative which emerges through the question of being.[16] The interrogative in question is neglected (i.e. ignored) by operative concepts, inasmuch as what is assumed as the reason on the ground of which operative concepts are established in the first place, is presupposed as an absolute given. What is presupposed as an absolute given appears to be beyond question, and therefore it remains unseen with regard to its origin, its derivation, and the fact that it is assumed, that is, with regard to the implications of its hypothetical character. What is presupposed as an absolute given, and thus assumed unquestioningly as "contingent ground", serves as the basis on which the certainty of truth is established in order to verify correct propositions about "contingent beings".[17] As a consequence, the question of being, as well as the interrogative which emerges through it, is not considered to be necessary. Quite the contrary! The answer to the question of being is apparently given by the presupposition of a "contingent ground". Furthermore, the question of being is considered to be disturbing, inasmuch as it appears to be ineffective within functional contexts and performs no effectivity with regard to their maintenance. This is to say that operability-based responsibility is characterized by the circumstance that it presupposes an obligation that is considered, without further ado, as the reason on the ground of which human practices ought to be based in order to be responsible in operative terms. As this ground is assumed as an absolute given, it is beyond question, and therefore serves as the "contingent ground" of the kind of conceptualization characteristic of operative concepts.

Even though end-in-itself-based responsibility also refers to an obligation which is assumed as the reason on the ground of which concepts of responsibility can be established, this obligation is not presupposed as an absolute given beyond question and therefore capable of serving as a "contingent ground". Rather, the obligation is assumed as response to the interrogative which emerges through the question of being. This can be seen, if we consider the circumstance that the obligation is assumed, that is, that its character is hypothetical. Thus, the assumption of this obligation does not go without saying but must be sustained by providing a reason on the basis of which it appears to be justified or even necessary. Once again, the quoted passage from Kant's *Inquiry into the Distinctness of the Principles of Natural Theology and Morals* offers some clarity on the subject. As already stated, Kant assumes a true obligation based on the notion of an end-in-itself. He assumes that an obligation must be necessary in itself in order to be a reliable ground for the establishment of the ethical character of true human practices. Even the guiding question of the modern metaphysical ethics—"What ought I to do?"—would come to nothing without such a reliable ground, because no "ought to" could be assumed, and consequently each answer to this question would be as good as any other. Therefore, Kant argues that the "the first formal ground of any necessity to act" (Kant, UD, AA 02: A96–97) is to:

> [...] Unterlasse das, wodurch die durch dich größtmögliche Voll—kommenheit verhindert wird.
>
> (Kant, UD, AA 02: A96–97)

> [...] abstain from doing that which will hinder the realization of the greatest achievable accomplishment.[18]

The assumed "end-in-itself" in terms of an "achievable accomplishment" is "the first formal ground of any necessity to act": this is to say that, on the one hand, the end-in-itself offers a reason on the grounds of which human beings are expected to establish their practices, and, on the other hand, the offered reason implies this ground in the form of a "necessity to act", that is, in the form of an obligation that contains within itself the need for a human response. In other words: all this is true under the condition that there is an "ought to" which is sustained in and through the being of man, while man takes a stance in the midst of beings. In the same textual passage, Kant further clarifies this point:

> Und hier finden wir, dass eine solche oberste Regel aller Verbind—lichkeit schlechterdings unerweislich sein müsse. Denn es ist aus keiner Betrachtung eines Dings oder Begriffs, welche es auch sei, möglich zu erkennen und zu schließen, was man tun soll, wenn dasjenige, was vorausgesetzt ist, nicht ein Zweck und die Hand—lung ein Mittel ist. Dies aber muß es nicht sein, weil es als dann keine Formel der Verbindlichkeit, sondern der problematischen Geschicklichkeit sein würde.
>
> (Kant, UD, AA 02: A96–97)

> And here we find that such an immediate supreme rule of all obligation must be absolutely indemonstrable. For it is impossible, by contemplating a thing or a concept of any kind whatever to recognize or infer what one ought to do, if that which is presupposed is not an end, and if the action is a means. But this cannot be the case, for if it were, our reason would not be a formula of obligation; it would be a formula of problematic skills.[19]

Any presupposed "ought to" must be traced back; that is, it must be reduced to a reason that, according to Kant, cannot be "recognized" or "inferred" "by contemplating things or concepts". How can it then be recognized, if ever? According to Kant, the required reduction is fulfilled through the assumption of a reason in terms of an end in itself. This is to say that the means-end rationality is not capable, on its own terms, to sustain any ethically relevant "ought to" if not through a presupposed obligation that is necessary in itself. All other forms of the "ought to" are mere recommendations because in and of themselves they do not offer a sufficient measure, a sufficient orientation for human practices. They are insufficient inasmuch as, through them, only man's own will to realize willingly established ends emerges, whereas nothing is said about the relation to being which man necessarily bares by being the being he is, by being a human being. Within the metaphysical tradition of ethics, "being a human being" means "becoming a human being". As a consequence, the question of a sufficient measure and orientation for human practices appears to be fundamental. According to Kant, the sufficient measure and orientation for human practices is established in light of the "ought to" and based on an obligation necessary in itself. The relation to being requires freedom: it requires the freedom to assume an obligation necessary in itself on the basis of which, now, human practices may be considered as accomplishable. In other words, only through an obligation necessary in itself is a sufficient reason for the establishment of the "ought to" offered, and thus a measure as well as an orientation for free human practices becomes likely.[20] As a consequence, the reason on the ground of which an obligation necessary in itself could be assumed is, by no means, a "contingent ground" but a ground that can be put into question and therefore involves an interrogative. Kant's answer to this interrogative says the following: if such a reason can be assumed, it has to be assumed in terms of an end in itself. If not so, the reason on the ground of which the "ought to" is assumed would not allow for a "formula of obligation" but would simply allow for a "formula of problematic skills". Thus, the assumption of a true obligation is in itself, according to Kant, already a response—namely, a response sustained in and through the being of man, while man takes a stance with regard to being in the midst of beings. This stance has to be taken with regard to the aforementioned interrogative. So, it is explicitly taken through a response to the question of being, which, however, is neglected (ignored) in operative concepts. In other words, what is assumed—through the question of being—is an "ought to" which determines the being of man as well as the being of beings. As this response is not assumed in the sense of an absolute given, but as the result of a response to the question of being, it is characteristic of ontological concepts, that is, of concepts that, in literal terms, "say being" (cf. De Gennaro 2019, 15).

As already stated (see p. 12 f.), the here-introduced distinction between operative concepts and ontological concepts is supposed to reduce responsibility to its ethical dimension, where, by ethical dimension, we mean the dimension that originally welcomes and ultimately sustains *human* dwelling, in a *human* "reality". This notion of "ethical dimension" is derived from the original sense of the Greek word ἦθος [ēthos], which indicates the habitual residence of man. In truth, ἦθος [ēthos] indicates the abode of men in the sense of the dimension which allows for and welcomes human dwelling (cf. Liddell, Scott 1996, 766). The attempt to understand this dimension and what concerns it, bore the name of ἐπιστήμη ἠθική [epistēme ēthikē] (cf. Heidegger 1994, 199); through the thinking of Heraclitus and Aristotle, that understanding constitutes the birthplace of ethics itself (cf. Zaccaria 1999, 88).

> ἦθος heißt Wohnung, Aufenthalt. Wir sagen: das Wohnen des Menschen, sein Aufenthalt inmitten des Seienden im Ganzen.
>
> (Heidegger 1994, 214)

> ἦθος means dwelling, abode. We say: the dwelling of the human being, his abode in the midst of beings in the whole.

This is, to the present day, the latent core of ethics, both in its ancient and its modern form, and in the form of applied moral science. The theory of virtue and the theory of value are expressions of this understanding of ethics (cf. Heidegger 1994, 200), which has its origin in the interrogative that allows for an understanding of the aforementioned dimension in terms of a response to the question of being. And it is this understanding which provides the frame within which the notion of responsibility became a key concept of ethics (cf. De Gennaro, Lüfter 2018, 145). As a consequence, ethical questions are supposed to unearth a dimension which allows for and welcomes human dwelling "on earth under the sky", offering a truly human "dwelling" in the midst of beings in the whole.

We see now, in retrospect, how operative concepts are in need of recourse to ontological concepts, so as to be founded. Operative concepts are in need of a recourse to the interrogative borne in the guiding question of the tradition of philosophy: What is being?[21] As a consequence, it can be said that if we are aiming for a conceptualization of responsibility which does not ignore its own ontological dimension, and therefore its ethical reason, we must take our cue from responses to the aforementioned question.

Notes

1 For obvious reasons, the conceptualization of responsibility in operative terms, as set out above, depends on the possibility to distinguish events that appear to be problematic from events that do not. Without this possibility, neither the problem-solving nor the problem-preventing potential of the notion of responsibility can come into play and, even less, be used effectively.

2 The *Oxford English Dictionary* defines "responsibility" as the "capability to fulfill an obligation".

3 At the moment, a distinction between two kinds of responsibility is emerging: (1) operability-based responsibility, i.e. responsibility based on an operative obligation; (2) end-in-itself-based responsibility, i.e. responsibility based on an obligation derived from an end in itself. The latter will be dealt with below in the discussion of modern (and in particular Kantian) ethics. However, a third kind of responsibility can also be conceived, namely, one which is based on the response to being itself, where the latter is, in turn, not conceived as an end in itself, but as having in itself the need for a human response, i.e. the need of being sustained in and through the being of man. This third kind of responsibility, which does not give rise to an obligation, will be referred to below (p. 21 f) as being-related responsibility.

4 In the context of this book, the expressions "metaphysical tradition of ethics" and "metaphysical ethics" refer to an explicit determination of the being of beings, i.e. to the guiding question of philosophy.

5 According to Nietzsche's diagnosis of this tradition, the idea of a highest truth is the birthplace of what he recognizes as "morality". By "morality", he usually means a system of value-posing within which a transcendental truth is assumed as the source of sense which determines each being in what it is in the first place. This system allows for the idea of a highest truth in terms of a highest value, by building on the notion of an individual who wills himself as the "good" man and therefore erects transcendental ideas that demand fulfillment. By virtue of his good will, he establishes morally responsible practices. Nietzsche considers his own philosophy as the overcoming of this kind of morality and thus as the overcoming of a tradition that he himself considers intrinsically "nihilistic". In fact, in his interpretation, nihilism is a destructive phenomenon that must be wholly accepted and "lived through" completely in order to be finally overcome. Therefore, Nietzsche speaks of himself as the first accomplished nihilist. According to Nietzsche, within the above-mentioned tradition, the idea of the highest truth, formulated in terms of a highest (absolute, eternal, supernatural) value, was adopted as a remedy for nihilism, whereas in truth, it provided no such remedy; on the contrary, from the very beginning, it carried in itself the seed of a new nihilism, which is the one whose rise Nietzsche himself experiences in his own epoch. The idea of a highest truth in terms of a highest value was the means by which, in the course of this tradition, attempts were undertaken to make sense of the becoming of the world, which, for itself, is completely senseless. In light of Nietzsche's concept of the will to power, the will that wills the good man responds to the will to power while not assuming it as such; in fact, it responds to the

will to power by negating that same will. Thus, the will that wills the good man, and therefore wills the good to be the highest truth, is the intrinsically nihilistic moral will that must be overcome (cf. Heidegger 1998, 103). In *Jenseits von Gut und Böse* [*Beyond Good and Evil*], Nietzsche states, "Es ist nicht mehr als ein moralisches Vorurteil, daß Wahrheit mehr wert ist als Schein." (KSA 5/34) — "It is no more than a moral prejudice that truth is worth more than semblance". Recalling Nietzsche's diagnoses is useful in the present context insofar as his position can be seen, arguably, as both the last ethical position, and as a preparation for the transition to an ethics that is no longer metaphysical (this is what is referred to above as being-based responsibility). On the other hand, his notion of the will to power sheds light on the operability-based notion of responsibility. In fact, when responsibility calls for operating for the sake of operating, this responsibility can be seen as an implementation of the will to power, or rather its evolution, the will to will.

6   Considering this constellation, and drawing on his concept of morality (cf. p. 6), Nietzsche refers to the "good man" as the "slave of the future". Posing the idea of a highest truth in terms of a highest value that ought to be actualized in the first place, and the superelevation of this value into the transcendental dimension, results in a constant decrease in the strength of the human being with regard to its capacity to bear what actually is, to wit the will to power (Heidegger 1998, 103).

7   Trans. by Paul Guyer and Allen W. Wood (Kant 1998).

8   Trans. by Paul Guyer and Allen W. Wood (Kant 2003).

9   Trans. by Paul Guyer and Allen W. Wood (Kant 2003).

10   Trans. by Paul Guyer and Allen W. Wood (Kant 2003).

11   Trans. by Paul Guyer and Allen W. Wood (Kant 2003).

12   See below p. 23 f.

13   See above, p. 4 f.

14   This is to say, an obligation which, in the absence of an end in itself, is an obligation based on the circumstance that it is functional to the achievement of mere effects (cf. p. 4 f.). This kind of obligation is not derived from a principle of perfection, which therefore cannot serve as a source for the accomplishment of each being; rather, it informs the deficiency of each being.

15   This is to say, an obligation which, in relation to an end in itself, is an obligation based on the circumstance that it is derived from a principle of perfection, which serves as source for the accomplishment of each being (cf. p. 6).

16   The question of being is referred to as the guiding question of the entire metaphysical tradition, i.e. the tradition of philosophy. It unites the four questions that are assumed to be characteristic of all philosophical endeavors from Plato to Nietzsche: What is the being of beings? (What is their essence?); What is truth? (Not in the sense of what is true, but in the sense of what is the sense of truth, that is: What does "to be true" mean?); What is man? (What is the essence of men?); What is the right measure? (What gives the measure to men and how can man assume that measure so that man's existence is a dignified one?). In other words: each fundamental endeavor within the philosophical tradition can be traced back to those four questions and eventually to the guiding question, "What is being?"

(Cf. Heidegger 1998, 251 f.; Zaccaria 2017). It has to be noted that the "tradition of philosophy" must not be confused with the "history of philosophy". One has little to do with the other. Tradition does not refer to a mere chronological sequence of theoretical positions that are distinguishable from and comparable to each other according to their occurrence in history. Neither is it the subject of reconstructions that describe the above-mentioned sequence by merely installing theoretical positions in an explicable order. Tradition, literally speaking, refers to "being handed down", "being handed over", "being transmitted". Since philosophy's rootedness in the question of being is fundamental to its tradition, and since this tradition is generated by asking this question, it can be said that the interrogative that requires the question of being is the constant source of philosophy. It is precisely this interrogative that, through ever-renewed responses to the question of being, is "handed down", is "handed over", and thereby is "transmitted".

17 The notion of "contingency" ("contingent ground", "contingent being") is discussed in depth at a later stage of the present text (see below, p. 27 f.).

18 Trans. by Paul Guyer and Allen W. Wood (Kant 2003).

19 Trans. by Paul Guyer and Allen W. Wood (Kant 2003).

20 Here and now, we do not have the opportunity to introduce Kant's concept of freedom and therefore to discuss his concept of action. However, it can be said that, according to Kant, the concept of action is not limited to human practices alone but includes also the realm of nature. In the *Critique of the Pure Reason,* Kant speaks about "Naturhandlungen", i.e. "nature actions" (cf. Kant, KrV A 548 / B 576.). This is to say that Kant's concept of action is based on causality and, as a consequence, related to the actualization of causal effects. Schematically speaking, what distinguishes "human actions" from "nature actions" is the fact that the former are brought about as humane practices through freedom, whereas the latter do not involve freedom. "Praktisch ist alles, was durch Freiheit möglich ist" (Kant, KrV B 828); "All that which is likely through freedom, is practical" (trans. by Paul Guyer and Allen W. Wood. Kant 1998). In fact, within the modern metaphysical tradition of philosophy, the notion of freedom is discussed in terms of causality, namely, as a form of causality.

21 In the context of this book, however, Kant's answer to the question of being is understood in light of Heidegger's reading of Kant (c.f. 1994[a], 1998[b]). Thereby, it should be noted that Heidegger's "Seinsfrage" and Kant's "question of being" are abyssal different.

3   Reduction to the necessary

As already stated at the beginning of this study, the focus of the present research is on a sufficiently distinctive characterization of the ethical dimension implied, though not always explicitly worked out, in the conceptualization of economic responsibility. The intent is therefore neither to provide a reflection on the correctness of already existing concepts of economic responsibility nor to ameliorate the basilar orientation of these concepts. This study will instead confine itself to an attempt to show how the reduction of concepts of economic responsibility to the fundamental questions of the tradition of philosophy restores their intrinsic ethical sense. Thus, the intent is to provide a contribution to the ongoing academic discourse by reducing the conceptualization of economic responsibility to the interrogative on which it is built in the first place. In other words, the present research will attempt to reduce the conceptualization of economic responsibility to the necessary. However, the expression "reduce to the necessary" should not be understood in terms of "diminishing" or "condensing" either the form or the content of economic responsibility, in order to obtain a generally applicable concept, but in terms of "bringing back", that is, bringing economic responsibility back to the dimension which allows for the restoration of its intrinsic ethical sense.

Accordingly, this research distinguishes between operative concepts of economic responsibility, on the one hand, and ontological concepts of economic responsibility, on the other hand. Whenever operative concepts are merely applied within a predefined functional context, the reduction of economic responsibility to its originating interrogative is suspended so that the necessary reduction of operative concepts to ontological concepts falls into oblivion. Oblivion, as it is meant here, is twofold, in that not only is the necessity of the reduction forgotten, but also the oblivion as such. That is the case of those concepts which are introduced in light of obligations which are not necessary in themselves, and have been defined as second-order obligations or simple recommendations. As a result of the twofold oblivion, these latter obligations obliterate the originating interrogative, in that they appear to be of the first order and to be necessary in themselves, when in fact they are not. Only adequate questions can let the originating interrogative emerge as such, in as far as these questions are capable of unearthing what is, in and of itself, open to further questioning, and therefore in constant need of the free capability to respond to it, that is, in constant need of true responsibility. Only through adequate questions is the interrogative itself assumed as the reason on the basis of which every conceptualization of economic responsibility rests in the first place. That is the case of those concepts which are introduced in light of an obligation necessary in itself, and which therefore, according to Kant, are of the first order. Thus, the conceptualization of responsibility remains bound to the reason on the grounds of which such an obligation can be assumed.

As can be easily noted, it is not a given that the notion of responsibility is defined as "capability to fulfill an obligation" (cf. *Oxford English Dictionary*) and therefore is related to what, in itself and out of itself, presupposes its actualization in terms of an imperative. The guiding question of modern, metaphysical ethics—"What ought I to do?"—refers to such an obligation in terms of what ought to be actualized in the first place through human practice. The obligation is thereby assumed as a principle of action which wills its own actualization and therefore implements itself as the source of sense for each being. As such, the obligation orients human practices and sets the tone for human relations with things, with nature, with other humans, with humankind itself—in one word: with that which is, or, as we can also say, with beings as such and in whole. So in the light of this obligation, there emerges a discrepancy between what ought to be (actualized) and what is (actual), which is fundamental to the constitution of modern metaphysical ethics and has its roots in the tradition of philosophy. It was precisely the aforementioned definition of responsibility which brought us to the distinction between "operability-based responsibility" (as emerging, for example, in light of the operability imperative) and "end-in-itself-based responsibility" (as emerging, for example, in light of Kant's categorical imperative). A third kind of responsibility is excluded from the aforementioned definition—namely, that kind of responsibility which was characterized as "being-related" in so far as it contains within itself the need for a human response that is not based on any obligation and thus not subject to any imperative, but related instead to the interrogative that emerges through the question of being. This is to say, that "being-related responsibility" is not based on what is fundamental to the constitution of modern metaphysical ethics—namely, the assumption of an "ought to" that is sustained by an obligation. It therefore follows that "being-related responsibility" is in and of itself the promise of a thinking that is born as and into the overcoming of the constraints of metaphysical ethics.

3.1 Constraints of Being

In an illuminating text titled *Einführung in die Metaphysik* [*Introduction to Metaphysics*], based on a lecture course held at the University of Freiburg i. Br. during the summer semester of 1935, Martin Heidegger indicates four, as he calls them, "Beschränkungen des Seins", that is four constraints to which being as such was subjected throughout the tradition of metaphysics: Being and becoming, Being and seeming, Being and thinking, Being and "ought to".[1] According to Heidegger, the latter constraint, while having been prefigured by the characterization of the ὄν as ἀγαθόν, is peculiar to modernity (cf. Heidegger 1998[a], 72),[2] and thus peculiar to the tradition of modern metaphysical ethics. Without delving into the development of his argumentation, it can be argued that lifting this constraint would allow for a fundamental redefinition of the notion of responsibility, which then would no longer be conceived in terms of the "capability to fulfill an obligation" but rather in terms of the "capability to respond to Being as such" (or Being itself). This, however, would inaugurate a yet untrodden path of interrogation regarding the notion of responsibility. This path is precisely what is supposed to be tentatively indicated by the introduced formula "being-related responsibility".

3.2 One foot in the air

The much-discussed theories of John Maurice Clark (1916), Milton Friedman (1970), and Archie B. Carroll (1979)[3] exemplify the application of operative concepts of the notion of economic responsibility to predefined functional contexts, and therefore offer an opportunity for the aforementioned reduction of responsibility to its ethical dimension. None of these theorists, however, addresses questions of ethical relevance in an explicit way, although their contributions do implicitly respond to these questions, and these implicit responses are fundamental to their concepts of responsibility. This conjuncture is essential, as that which is constitutive of the notion of economic responsibility from the outset, and hence remains fundamental to each of their attempts of conceptualization, has been introduced unquestioningly, that is, without any explicit reference to its originating interrogative.[4] This is to say that each of their attempts of conceptualization assumes the aforementioned definition of the notion of responsibility as "capability to fulfill an obligation" (cf. *Oxford English Dictionary*), whereas none of them puts this assumption into question. So, on the one hand, they build on an understanding of responsibility which is derived from the tradition of modern metaphysical ethics, whereas, on the other hand, these attempts neglect (ignore) the elementary distinction between the notion of operability-based responsibility and end-in-itself-based responsibility. In fact, in the context of Clark's, Friedman's, and Carroll's concepts of economic responsibility, this distinction is of no importance. Obligations—of economic as well as of political, social, ethical character—are presupposed as given and compared to one another without further ado. In other words, obligations are presupposed as available and comparable "contingent grounds"[5] without becoming explicit as such in their questionable constitution. The consequence is that only operative concepts of economic responsibility have been established so far. What is more, they have been established without the awareness of their highly operative character. As already stated earlier,[6] operative concepts are in need of recourse to ontological concepts, so as to be sufficiently founded. Consequently, operative concepts of economic responsibility, which remain without recourse to their ontological implications, and therefore are not reduced to their ethical dimension, "are always having"— to use a Kantian expression—"one foot in the air" (Kant, KrV A 467 / B 495). They are established without a sufficient reason on the ground of which they can be assumed.

3.3 The premise of reason

In order to be able to discern the implications of the already outlined conjuncture, one must first recognize the role assigned to the so-called "premise of reason" within the tradition of metaphysics. In this regard, the introductory notes of a lecture course, held by Martin Heidegger in the winter semester 1955/1956 at the University of Freiburg, lend a helping hand:

> [Sodass] der menschliche Verstand selbst überall und stets, wo und wann er tätig ist, alsbald nach dem Grund Ausschau hält, aus dem das, was ihm begegnet, so ist, wie es ist. Der Verstand schaut nach dem Grund aus, insofern er selbst, der Verstand nämlich, die Angabe des Grundes verlangt. Der Verstand fordert Be-gründung

für seine Aussagen und Behauptungen. [...] Das menschliche Vorstellen trachtet in all dem, wovon es umgeben ist und angegangen
wird, nach Gründen, oft nur nach den nächstliegenden, bisweilen
auch nach den weiter zurückliegenden, schließlich nach den ersten
und letzten Gründen.

(Heidegger 2006, 13)

[Thus] human understanding, wherever and whenever it is engaged, always and steadily looks out for the reason for which what
encounters it, is, as it is. Understanding looks out for reason insofar as it [i.e. understanding] requires, on its own terms, a state-
ment of reason. Understanding requires the reduction-to-reason
of propositions and assumptions. [...] In all that encompasses and
concerns them, the human representations seek reasons, often just
the very proximate ones, occasionally even the more remote ones,
finally the first and last reasons.[7]

The lecture course from which this quotation is taken is titled *Der Satz
vom Grund* [*The Principle of Reason*] and is dedicated primarily to the
principle of sufficient reason which, in its shortened form, reads: *nihil
est sine ratione*, that is, nothing is without reason. Concerning the thus
formulated principle, Heidegger writes:

"Diese Fassung spricht in der lateinischen Sprache. Der Satz vom
Grund wurde in dieser Fassung zum ersten Mal im Umkreis der-
jenigen Besinnungen erreicht und besonders erörtert, die Leibniz im 17. Jahrhundert geglückt sind. Die Philosophie waltet und
wandelt sich jedoch im Abendland bereits seit dem 6. vorchristli-
chen Jahrhundert. Demnach dauert es zweitausenddreihundert
Jahre, bis das abendländisch-europäische Denken dahin gelangte,
den einfachen Satz vom Grund zu finden und aufzustellen. Wie
seltsam, daß ein so naheliegender Satz, der unausgesprochen alles menschliche Vorstellen und Verhalten überall lenkt, so viele
Jahrhunderte gebraucht hat, um eigens als Satz in der genannten
Fassung ausgesprochen zu werden. Aber noch seltsamer ist es, daß
wir uns immer noch nicht darüber wundern, mit welcher Lang-
samkeit der Satz vom Grund zum Vorschein kommt. Man möchte
die lange Zeit, die er dazu brauchte, seine Incubationszeit nennen:
zweitausenddreihundert Jahre für das Setzen dieses einfachen
Satzes. Wo und wie hat der Satz vom Grund so lange geschlafen
und das in ihm Ungedachte vorausgeträumt?

(Heidegger 2006, 14 f.)

This formulation speaks in Latin. The formulation of the principle of reason was first achieved and considered in the context of those meditations Leibniz carried out in the seventeenth century. In the West, however, philosophy has been reigning and transforming itself ever since the sixth century BC. Hence it took two thousand three hundred years until Western European thinking actually discovered and formulated the simple principle of reason. How odd that such an obvious principle, which always directs all human cognition and conduct without being stated, needed so many centuries to be expressly stated as principle in the formulation cited above. But it is even odder that we never wonder about the slowness with which the principle of reason came to light. One would like to call the long time it needed for this its 'incubation period': two thousand three hundred years for the posing of this simple preposition. Where and how did the principle of reason sleep for so long and presciently dream what is unthought in it?[8]

While it is beyond the scope of the present research to attempt an answer to this question and to engage in an in-depth investigation of the far-reaching implications of Leibniz' *principium rationis*, for the purposes of this research, the following assumption will be made: as long as the concept of ethics rests upon the premise of reason, as claimed by the principle of reason, the notion to which all human practices are entrusted is the notion of an available reason for all, whose actualization is attainable in the form of its being present, its being likely, and its being necessary. Within the tradition of philosophy, the availability of this reason is ultimately based on a withdrawal (namely, the withdrawal of being which presents itself as interrogative through the question of being, i.e. through the guiding question of philosophy) on the grounds of which any true responsibility is established in the first place. This is to say that the reason on the grounds of which ethically relevant obligations are established is assumed with regard to an originating interrogative that requires, in order to be assumed as such, the free capability to respond to it by assuming an interrogating stance which is aware of the necessity of responding to the question of being. Previously in this text, we characterized this necessity by drawing on the distinction between operative and ontological concepts, and by showing how operative concepts are in need of recourse to ontological concepts, that is, to concepts that "say being", that is, to concepts that assume in and of themselves an interrogating stance with regard to being.

In other words, by assuming an interrogating stance, the reason on the grounds of which responsibility is built is experienced as withdrawal of being—that is, as the originating interrogative—and must be adopted and sustained as such in order to be grounded. This means that what is actual can be said truthfully on the condition that the reason for its actuality is understood as something available to human knowledge through questioning; that what is likely can be said truthfully on the condition that the reason for its likelihood is understood as something available to human knowledge through questioning; that what is necessary can be said truthfully on the condition that the reason for its necessity is understood as something available to human knowledge through questioning.

It was already stated[9] that, within the tradition of metaphysical ethics, the aforementioned reason is assumed in terms of a principle of perfection that serves as a constant source of the likely accomplishment of each being. Each being, merely by virtue of its relation to such a principle, appears to be perfectible and therefore appears to await a human practice through which it could be awakened in its attendance to sustain the actualization of the greatest achievable accomplishment. According to Kant, the first formal ground of any ethically relevant obligation lies precisely in this actualization which, in turn, can be considered to be the determinant of any true responsibility. This holds true for economic responsibility as well as social responsibility, political responsibility, responsibility in the sciences and technical sectors, and so forth. It is, however, decisive to see how, within the tradition of ethics, the reference to the aforementioned interrogative is preserved, so that the reason on the grounds of which, for example, principles of perfection are introduced, remains open to question. Thus, concepts of responsibility derived from that originating interrogative are ontological concepts. They are ontological concepts in as far as they preserve the originating interrogative which eventually emerges with the question of being—that is, with the guiding question of the philosophical tradition within which ethics constituted a response to the interrogative as such.

The character of the premise of reason changes radically with the introduction of operative concepts. What appears to be knowable through these concepts is understood on a contingent basis, which is assumed in such a way that, on the one hand, it establishes a predefined scope within which beings become available, and, on the other hand, it excludes, and consequently neglects, the originating interrogative in as much as it disturbs their operative functionality. Beings represented on the basis of a contingent ground are themselves contingent. This is to say that operative concepts of responsibility are no longer built on the originating interrogative that is assumed in an interrogating stance. Rather, they are built on a contingent ground that is assumed as an absolute given, that is, as a brute fact which, as such, is beyond question. A responsible stance in which man responds to contingent beings is characterized by the immediacy of its response. It can thus be called "responsive", and in this way distinguished from responsibility based on an "ontological mediation". Responsive decisions, for example, are characterized by the fact that they do not involve a judgment concerning the true sense of beings but tend to turn into automatized reactions to contingent beings. Responsive decisions are, so to speak, irresponsible with regard to the reason on the basis of which an ontological concept of responsibility—that is, an ontological concept of responsible decision—could be built. What is assumed as an absolute given is not in need of further questioning and therefore excluded from the necessity of any further reduction-to-reason.

3.4 Contingent ground and entruing element

In order to understand the radical change that takes place with the introduction of operative concepts of responsibility, one must first consider the peculiar rootlessness of contingent beings.[10] Contingent beings are, in the first place, characterized by contingency. Contingency is the peculiar manner of being which occurs, and appears, within an operative context, including the context of our everyday life; as such, it characterizes

> what is always in the foreground in a pressing manner, what is due before anything else, insisting that something be done with it or in response to it. The peculiar contact with such 'things' tends to fill up all time and all space; in fact, it has its own time and space, which is a time and space of 'doing' [effecting]; that is, an *operative* time and space... [W]e take [the word contingency] – which commonly means an accident or an unforeseen and unforeseeable event – to indicate the character of immediate (viz. unmediated) impact of things, namely the direct impact on our (inert) life-sphere or 'lived experience'.
>
> (De Gennaro 2019, 65)

In what impacts our life-sphere in this manner, the sense-element of things (i.e. the being of beings) is, so to speak, conflated with things themselves; in other words, the impact of contingency on our life-sphere follows the disappearance of the difference between a thing and its sense (or: between a being and its being). As a consequence, "in the encounter with what is contingent, the sense of that which is reduced to contingency is not interrogated, not sustained in knowledge, and thus not clarified" (De Gennaro 2019, 65). The operative concepts of science are based on contingency; scientific knowledge, insofar as it is based on contingency, is knowledge (a functional theory) of contingency. (See also the related elucidation of likelihood, p. X).

A contingent being is assumed as an already constituted being, which is supposed to persist independently from the existence of human beings. Its persistence is assumed as an absolute given that can be taken for granted and consequently represented by the human being without any further necessity for questioning. A contingent being is an integral part of an already constituted, contingent reality within which human beings live and to which human beings are constantly related. All experiences of this reality, and of all beings contained in this reality, appear to be representable in terms of cause-effect relationships. With regard to the human being, it can be said that all experiences which can be made of this reality and of the beings contained in it, have the character of "lived impacts". The word "impact", again, refers to the immediacy that characterizes these experiences, even when that which is experienced has been previously objectivized by means of a scientific conceptualization (c.f. Zaccaria 2017[a]). For example, the physicochemical constitution of a tree is supposed to persist independently of the existence of the human being. What is more, it is also supposed to be the reason on the grounds of which the tree can be experienced in the first place. This is to say that the physicochemical constitution of the tree is assumed as a subsistent reason, thanks to which the tree is represented by man as rooted in the earth, as soaring into the sky, as wide and uneven, as solid and deep green, and so forth. All these appear to be mere properties of an "object tree". In fact, it seems that we are looking at mere properties of what is a physicochemical reality in the first place, whose physicochemical reality appears to be the very reason on the grounds of which it has properties in the first place, and whose physicochemical reality appears to be the reason on the grounds of which human beings are able to experience it in the first place. Thus, the physicochemical reality is assumed as the contingent reason on the grounds of which the tree is available for human representations in the first place.

By looking more closely at what is in sight here, one becomes aware of the fact that a concrete, single tree is experienced as a contingent tree, as the consequence of a preceding operation. This is to say that the concrete, single tree is considered in light of an isolated trait common to all trees: its measurable and computable physicochemical reality. This reality is assumed to be the tree's substance, that is, its "truth". In other words, the phenomenon "tree" (i.e. its integrity as a whole sense-relations) is reduced to its measurable and computable physicochemical reality, which then becomes the abstract substance of each concrete tree. Undeniably, the physicochemical composition of a concrete, single tree cannot be negated—neither can its measurability and computability—but it does not go without saying that the said composition is to be assumed as the substance of the phenomenon "tree". Consequently, this operation is in itself questionable. The contingent tree is not just given in an absolute way but as the result of the indicated operation of objectivization, which can, in turn, be called into question (c.f. Zaccaria, 2017ᵃ). In this regard, Gino Zaccaria's *The Light of Cézanne* (2018) teaches us a lesson that we have yet to learn. Zaccaria quotes the following passage from a letter which Paul Cézanne wrote to his friend Èmile Zola on April 9, 1858:

"Do you remember that pine tree, planted on the banks of the Arc, which soared with its crowny top above the gaping abyss at its feet? That pine which, with its leaves, protected our bodies from the ardour of the sun—ah! may the Gods preserve it from the baleful assault of the logger's axe!

(c.i. Zaccaria 2018, 1)

Referring to this passage, Zaccaria comments:

[The artist] recalls the difference between the eye of the painter, for which the indoles of the pine is no mere indifferent, general concept, but rather the retracted origin of the uniqueness and singularity of this or of that tree, and that of the common vision is imposed by utility, according to which pine trees belong to the stock of so-called natural resources, and which shows a priori the character of being transformable into timber and firewood. The logger's axe cannot perceive the richness understood as flagrancy of the green colour in its contrast, on one hand, with the ardour of the sun and the celestial azure, and, on the other, with the darkness of the terrestrial abyss—a richness that is profusion and copiousness of truth. [...] We must therefore think of the painting *Le grand pin* as a way of letting go of the useable tree in order that the tree of flagrancy might be free, that it might clear [...]. The painting—which is not a 'reproduction' of a pine tree nor, much less, is a 'representation', but rather an entruing[11] of its being— imposes a transformation of the common vision (the eye of the 'lived impact' and of contingency) in pictorial seeing: that seeing which refers and is dedicated solely to the truth. Indeed, Cézanne will write in his famous 'promise' to Émile Bernard that 'Je vous dois la vérité en peinture et je vous la dirai' [...].

(2018, 1)

What emerges here is the true responsibility of the painter, consisting in the always unique capability of a human being to respond to the flagrancy of light without assuming it through operative concepts as a contingent phenomenon that can be used in the functional context of mere art production. It is the first and the only responsibility of the painter to assume an interrogating stance toward the originating interrogative so as to bring it to light as the entruing element of painting.

Operative concepts assume the availability of contingent beings by presupposing a contingent ground that ascertains the possibility of a correct conceptualization of what is actual, of what is likely, and of what is necessary. This is to say that the ascertainment of any correct conceptualization depends on what is presupposed in its availability and therefore assumed as a contingent being, while the reason on the grounds of which this appears to be justified remains beyond question. Furthermore, the interrogative which requires the indicated justification does not even come into view. This is to say that the premise of reason is suspended through the unquestioned assumption of a presupposed contingent ground that ascertains the correct conceptualization of contingent beings through operative concepts. So, the "brute" contingent ground supplants the originating interrogative of ontological concepts and serves as a surrogate for the premise of reason as we know it from the philosophical tradition.

Philosophy, on the other hand, has unfolded in the tradition of the premise of reason by assuming the availability of a reason in the form of a ground on which conceptualizations become likely in the first place. According to this tradition, the premise of reason involves the availability of such a reason wherever and whenever man pursues knowledge. It is characteristic of man himself to pursue knowledge, not in the sense of collecting explanations about the world but in the sense of understanding the world by interrogating it. This is to say that there is no world without the understanding of man, and that there is no man without the understanding of world. Within the aforementioned tradition, such understanding builds on the premise of reason. Thereby, the premise of reason is experienced as withdrawal of being and therefore requires an interrogating stance through the explicit assumption of the question of being. This withdrawal allows for research in various fields of knowledge and orients the constant striving for reason on the ground of which true knowledge can be built. In this manner, what is pursued in the first place (i.e. a sufficient understanding of the relation to being in order to found site for man's dwelling) is achieved through questioning. What is achieved through questioning was adduced through reason. What is adduced through reason remains in itself questionable. What is in itself questionable requires a free capability to respond to it—in short, it requires man's true responsibility. In other words: according to the premise of reason, true knowledge requires the premise of an originating interrogative that serves as sufficient reason on the ground of which concepts may be built, which, in turn, can be reduced-to-reason. In the tradition of metaphysical ethics, as already stated, the sufficiency of reason was offered by what could serve as an end in itself, that is, by what could serve as a principle of perfection and thus as a source for the likely accomplishment of each being. Thereby, the aforementioned originating interrogative emerged through the question of being which in and of itself gathers the generation of ontological concepts. This is to say that in light of the philosophical understanding of the premise of reason, the rootedness of ontological concepts is hosted by the originating interrogative that emerges through the question of being.

Operative concepts, however, are different in kind, in that what appears through them remains contingent and thus, with regard to the indicated premise of reason, rootless. The premise of reason, as it was affirmed in the tradition of philosophy, gives rise to the notion of first and last reasons in terms of ontological concepts. In other words, the premise of reason is affirmed as its own reason, whereas operative concepts are not capable of responding to it. Wherever and whenever human understanding is based on a contingent ground, all derived operative concepts are not adduced through the reduction-to-reason and therefore are necessarily unjustified and in relation to ontological concepts, literally, irresponsible. In other words, the preclusion of ontological concepts on a contingent ground subjugates the premise of reason, inasmuch as the discontingent reason of any contingent ground remains equally unthought as contingency itself. What appears instead is an unquestioned ground that is supposed to be without the need of being adduced by reduction-to-reason, that is, a ground that is taken for granted as an absolute given. The circumstance that such a contingent ground was adduced remains unquestioned, along with the conditions of its adduction. In fact, this ground is unreasonably assumed to be the sense-giving and sense-determining origin of what is available in terms of knowable. The said ground stands for a preestablished reason that was introduced "without having been explicitly originated by and through the freedom of man" and thus even prepared to be "calculated as an effect of other contingent circumstances" (De Gennaro 2006, 84). Thereby, what is actual appears in light of its mere effectiveness, what is likely appears in light of its mere possibility,[12] and what is necessary appears in light of a linear causality. As a consequence, the knowable is prevalently seen in its calculable effectiveness, in its realizable possibility, in its provable causality.

Based on the aforementioned premise, only those concepts for which a sufficient reason can be adduced can be said to be true. In other terms, only for those concepts for which a reduction-to-reason is achievable does the claim to truth seem to be justified. According to this premise and to the distinction between operative concepts and ontological concepts, only the latter may be considered to be reasonable and consequently to be determined by reason (cf. Heidegger 2006, 196). Here, a second meaning of reason comes to light. Reason can be understood not only in the sense of a ground that accounts for … but also in the sense of the way in which man perceives that which is, by preserving it, thanks to its capability to respond to being and therefore to find site for his dwelling in the midst being in whole. Both meanings of reason are relevant for the present research on economic responsibility and the question of ethics. If we come back to the concept of responsibility that was already introduced in light of modern metaphysical ethics, we can see the following: what is perceived in the first place as a reasonable ground for responsible human practices is an obligation necessary in itself. This ground is assumed as the reason on which the conceptualization of responsibility is based in order to reduce the notion of responsibility to its ethical dimension. At the same time, this reasonable ground must be assumed by the human being, through the free capability to respond to the obligation necessary in itself. Reason, in its second meaning, is therefore understood neither as the mere human ability to perceive an obligation in the sense of a realizable end nor as a means to adopt, in an appropriate way, the right means to fulfill it. Rather, reason, in its second meaning, is then understood as what allows human beings to become what they are in the first place, that is, to become the being that in and of itself is determined by the relation to being and therefore is obliged to take each time a unique and incomparable stance in the midst of beings in the whole. It is through his own practices that the human being takes this stance and assumes his own being—namely, assumes the relation to being which in and of itself requires his response, requires its assumption by the human being, requires true responsibility.

Notes

1 Gleich wie wir im 'ist' eine durchaus geläufige Weise des Sein-Sagens antreffen, so stoßen wir bei der Nennung des Namens 'Sein' auf ganz bestimmte, schon formelhaft gewordene Weisen des Sagens: Sein und Werden; Sein und Schein; Sein und Denken; Sein und Sollen. [...] Wir verfolgen [...] die Unterscheidung des Seins gegen Anderes. Dabei sollen wir zwar erfahren, daß und das Sein entgegen der landläufigen Meinung alles andere als ein leeres Wort ist, vielmehr so vielseitig bestimmt, daß wir uns kaum zurechtfinden, um die Bestimmtheit genügend zu bewahren. Allein, das genügt nicht. (Heidegger 1998[a], 71)—

> Just as we find a thoroughly ordinary way to say Being in the 'is', we also find entirely determined manners of speaking that have already become formulaic in the naming of the name "Being": Being and becoming; Being and seeming; Being and thinking; Being and "ought to". [...] We will now pursue Being's distinctions against Other. In doing this, we will learn that, contrary to the widely accepted opinion, Being is anything but an empty word for us. Instead, it is determined in so multifaceted a fashion that we can hardly find our bearing to preserve this determination sufficiently. But this is not enough.
> (Trans. by Gregory Fried and Richard Polt, adapted by the author, Heidegger 2000[a])

2 Es bedarf jetzt keiner weitläufigen Erörterung, um noch eigens zu verdeutlichen, wie auch in dieser Scheidung das gegen das Sein Ausgeschiedene, das Sollen, nicht irgendsonstwoher dem Sein zu- und angetragen wird. Das Sein selbst bringt, und zwar in der bestimmten Auslegung als Idee, den Bezug zum Vorbild-haften und Gesollten mit sich. In dem Maße als das Sein selbst sich hinsichtlich seines Ideencharakters verfestigt, in dem gleichen Maße drängt es dazu, die damit geschehende Herabsetzung des Seins wieder wettzumachen. Aber das kann jetzt nur noch so gelingen, daß etwas *über* das Sein gesetzt wird, was das Sein stets noch nicht ist, aber jeweils sein *soll*. (Heidegger 1998[a], 150)—

> There is no need for far-reaching considerations now in order to make clear that also with this distinction, what is secerned from Being, the ought (to be), is not proposed and imposed on Being from the outside. Being itself, in its particular understanding as idea, brings with it the relation to the original ideal and to what ought to be. As Being itself is affirmed with regard to its character as idea, it also tends to make up for the ensuing degradation of Being. But now, this can occur only by setting something *above* Being that Being never yet is, but always *ought to be*.
> (Trans. by Gregory Fried and Richard Polt, adapted by the author, Heidegger 2000[a])

3 See p. 42 f.
4 It has already been shown in the first part of this book (see p. 12 f.) that any operative concept of economic responsibility is based on assumptions that, in their turn, respond to questions of ethical relevance. This is to say that ethical questions raise issues that necessitate the capability to

respond to them whenever and wherever economic responsibility is addressed and related concepts come up for discussion. The said issues are inherent to the notion of economic responsibility itself. In other words, operative concepts of economic responsibility are constituted in the form of, and can be read as response to, these questions.

5 See p. 27 f.
6 See p. 12 f.
7 Trans. by Reginald Lilly (Heidegger 1999).
8 Trans. by Reginald Lilly (Heidegger 1999).
9 See p. 6 f.
10 An illuminating clarification of the notion of contingency is provided by Gino Zaccaria in an interview titled *Tempo spazio arte* (2017[a]).
11 To entrue something is to restore and preserve it in its truth.
12 On the difference between likelihood and possibility, see p. 10, fn. 1.

4 The conceptualization of economic responsibility

The conceptualization of economic responsibility, as we know it from the aforementioned contributions of Clark (2016), Friedman (1970), and Carroll (1979), is operability-based and thus subject to the imperative of operability. This can be seen by considering the fact that all three authors assume a linear relationship between acting subjects and the effects of their action, and all three assume the simultaneous presence of different obligations that are related to different contexts of action according to which responsibility is each time defined depending on what appears to be necessary in order to sustain the contexts of action in their functionality. The obligations here assumed are not necessary in themselves and thus, according to Kant (see p. 9), mere recommendations. This is to say that, according to the tradition of metaphysical ethics, all those imperatives which are derived from mere recommendations are ethically irrelevant, as long as they are not based on a reason that provides in and of itself an end in itself. In fact, operative imperatives are defined by the context of action and relative to the functionality of the context of action.

4.1 Contextual economic responsibility

The following quotations illustrate how this circumstance conditions the conceptualization of economic responsibility and to what extent it allows exclusively for operability-based responsibility:

> In a free-enterprise, private-property system, a corporate executive is an employee of the owners of the business. He has direct responsibility to his employers. That responsibility is to conduct the business in accordance with their desires, which generally will be to make as much money as possible while conforming to their basic rules of the society, both those embodied in law and those

embodied in ethical custom [...] [T]he key point is that, in his capacity as a corporate executive, the manager is the agent of the
individuals who own the corporation or the eleemosynary institution, and his primary responsibility is to them.

(Friedman 1970)

Of course, the corporate executive is also a person in his own
right. As a person, he may have many other responsibilities that he
recognizes or assumes voluntarily—to his family, his conscience,
his feelings of charity, his church, his clubs, his city, his country.
He may feel impelled by these responsibilities to devote part of his
income to causes he regards as worthy, to refuse to work for particular corporations, even to leave his job, for example, to join his
country's armed forces. If we wish, we may refer to some of these
responsibilities as 'social responsibilities'. But in these respects he
is acting as a principal, not an agent; he is spending his own money
or time or energy, not the money of his employers or the time or
energy he has contracted to devote to their purposes. If these are
'social responsibilities', they are the social responsibilities of individuals, not business.

(Friedman 1970)

In light of the premise of reason, as was established within the tradition of ethics, the confinement of an obligation to a limited context
of action that appears to be reasonable, becomes an evident problem
insofar as actions may be considered responsible if context-dependent
conditions are accepted, whereas the very same actions may be considered to be less responsible, or even irresponsible, if some other conditions are considered to be more reasonable or the same conditions
are considered to be unreasonable. Hence, we find man exposed to
the situation of being unable to discern what in the first place requires
true responsibility. We find him unable to understand if an obligation
persists for good reasons or not, that is, whether it is a question of true
obligation or a question of mere recommendation. Thus, we see how
man is disoriented in the midst of beings, in the midst of the world,
as long as the reduction-to-reason is suspended. But this is only the
minor part of a much wider problem, which consists in the fact that
even by confining the context of action, concepts of economic responsibility already respond to implicit ethical questions, that is, questions that are principally related to the aforementioned originating
interrogative which bestows and allots the whole of sense-relations of
human existence. This is to say that operative decisions, yes, may be

confined to functional contexts, but only insofar as these functional contexts persist in the dimension of the whole of sense-relations, which therefore remain elemental for each human practice and are by no means suspended through the introduction of predefined functional contexts. Where these ethical questions do not emerge, all efforts to orient human practices by means of mere operative concepts turn out to be inert (and consequently blind) with regard to the interrogative which bestows and allots the whole of sense-relations and therefore remains the reason on the basis of which all operative concepts of economic responsibility, as well as all functional contexts within which these concepts are applied, ultimately rest. Operative concepts of economic responsibility depend on predefined functional contexts, established on arbitrary suppositions, with the result that relative decisions are insufficiently critical and therefore ethically blank (cf. Lüfter 2019, 105).

The problem was already raised earlier, when Kant's question concerning the first formal ground of ethics was discussed with regard to the guiding question of modern ethics: "What ought I to do?" (Kant, KrV, 804–805). Kant argues that no true obligation subsists if the necessity that demands a certain action refers merely to the choice of those means one ought to adopt toward a predefined end in order to realize it. The said end is predefined inasmuch as it is confined to a predetermined functional context so that the presumed obligation specifies a prescription as the solution to a problem which emerges exclusively as a result of the assumed end and context. Now, since no other necessity attaches to the employment of means than that which belongs to the mentioned end, all the actions which are prescribed under the conditions of certain ends are contingent. According to Kant, these obligations cannot be called obligations at all—at least, as long as they are not subordinated to an end which appears to be necessary in itself (cf. Kant, UD AA 02: A 96–97). Even though the notion of responsibility is not mentioned in the above-cited text passage of Kant's work, we may state that under the conditions of a determined functional context, within which contingent ends suggest the adoption of certain means, no true responsibility is needed insofar as there is nothing that ought to be fulfilled in the first place. The notion of responsibility is replaced by what may be indicated as mere responsiveness (cf. De Gennaro, Lüfter 2018). All established ends are adduced from a predefined functional context within which the premise of reason is suspended, as long as no end necessary in itself can be assumed. At this level, the emergence of ethical questions related to their originating interrogative is not achieved, and, according to Kant, only second-order imperatives are justified. This is to say, no true responsibility is likely.

Accordingly, the conceptualization of economic responsibility, as introduced thus far, is likewise informed by the imperative of operability and defined by a preestablished context of action and its functional requirements. Responsibility is then introduced as a suitable means for solving those problems that could emerge in the predefined context of economics with regard to those purposes that are preestablished as economic in nature. Responsibility is then expected to become applicable in the field of economics by developing its problem-solving and problem-preventing potential in the most effective way. The reason on the grounds of which operative concepts of economic responsibility appear to be reasonable is the aforementioned obligation that—being blind to the principle of perfection as we know it from the tradition of ethics—implements the constant imperfection of each being. The sense of everything that is, including human knowledge and human practices, is validated by and dependent on the degree to which these practices and knowledge are able to meet the demand of the imperative of operability. Therefore, constant imperfection becomes a matter of principle inasmuch as the imperative of operability implies the claim to utmost effectiveness which, in and of itself, is unable to provide any measure of sufficiency. Quite the contrary—in and of itself, it requires overcoming all achieved effectiveness, so that perfection is excluded from the outset. Sense (that which "makes sense") is derived exclusively from the capability to respond to the imperative of operability and thus from the capability to serve for the actualization of the imperative of operability by implementing a constantly elevated degree of a secured enhancement of effectiveness.

The imperative of operability that demands its actualization is cut off from any reference to accomplishment and therefore no longer concerned with the principle of perfection, that is, no longer concerned with what Kant proposed as the first formal ground of any obligation, and what was conceived, throughout the tradition of ethics, as an end in itself. On condition that the imperative of operability orients human practices, what ought to be in the first place is characterized as inherently unaccomplishable, as suffering a constant insufficiency. Consequently, human practices are seen as a means to carry out an effect: namely, the effect of eliminating a recurrent deficit of effectiveness, which, however, never brings us closer to any form of accomplishment. This is true even for operative concepts of economic responsibility as well as of social and political responsibility, among others.

4.2 No-man's-land of ethical theory

In this respect, Hans Jonas's text, *Das Prinzip Verantwortung. Versuch einer Ethik für die technologische Zivilisation* (*The imperative of responsibility. In search of an ethics for the technological age*), is paradigmatic. In the foreword to this text, published in 1979, Jonas delineates some of the circumstances of the rise of responsibility to become a key concept of ethics. The starting point for his reflection is an eminent menace that threatens human beings on the level of existence as well as on the level of essence and of freedom. The eminent menace is the result of a profound transformation process in various fields of human practice—first and foremost, transformation processes in the technical sphere whose development is based on scientific progress and driven by the restless quest for economic growth (Jonas 1979, 7). Jonas's text constitutes a transition from an ontological concept of responsibility, as outlined with reference to the tradition of ethics, to an operative concept of responsibility, as required by applied ethics. With regard to the aforementioned menace, responsibility assumes a prevalently responsive character, that is, the character of an immediate reaction to a contingent situation that is considered to be problematic. Jonas argues that a new kind of ethical position is needed as a response to an entirely unprecedented and unpredicted situation. The new ethical position, which is meant to surrogate the insufficiency of classical ethical reasoning within the tradition of philosophy, requires a new imperative which Hans Jonas calls the "ecological imperative":

> Was der Mensch heute tun kann und dann, in der unwiderstehlichen Ausübung dieses Könnens, weiterhin zu tun gezwungen ist, das hat nicht seinesgleichen in vergangener Erfahrung. Auf sie war alle bisherige Weisheit über rechtes Verhalten zugeschnitten. [...] Das Neuland kollektiver Praxis, das wir mit der Hochtechnologie betreten haben, ist für die ethische Theorie noch ein Niemandsland.
>
> (Jonas 1979, 7)

> What present-day man can do, and therefore, in the irresistible exercise of his power, is compelled to keep on doing, has no equivalent in past experiences. However, our entire wisdom concerning the proper way to be was tailored to those experiences. [...] The virgin land of collective practice, that we have begun to walk on with the advent of high technology, is still a no man's land for ethical theory.[1]

Jonas's imperative, which was formulated following Kant's categorical imperative, reads as follows:

> Handle so, dass die Wirkungen deiner Handlung verträglich sind mit der Permanenz echten menschlichen Lebens auf Erden.
>
> (Jonas 1979, 36)

> Act in a way that the consequences of your actions are compatible with the permanence of an authentically humane life on earth.[2]

Even though it seems as if the expression "authentically human life" invokes the aforementioned principle of perfection—which is characteristic of classical ethics, and is therefore rooted in the originating interrogative of the tradition of philosophy—it does not, and in fact turns out to be misleading. Jonas does not introduce any criterion of authenticity, and, what is more, he explicitly postpones the introduction of such a criterion insofar as the securing of the persistence of human life on earth has absolute priority. This is to say that authenticity is subordinated to the persistence of human life on earth and thus not introduced as a notion that has the status of a principle and can thus serve as the original source of sense.

> Für den Augenblick tritt alle Arbeit am "eigentlichen" Menschen zurück hinter die bloße Rettung der Voraussetzung dafür – der Existenz einer Menschheit in einer zugänglichen Natur. Von der immer offenen Frage, was der Mensch sein soll, deren Antwort wandelbar ist, sind wir in der totalen Gefahr des welthistorischen Jetzt zurückgeworfen auf das erste, jener Frage immer schon zugrundeliegende, aber bisher nie aktuell gewordene Gebot, daß er sein soll – allerdings als Mensch.
>
> (Jonas 1979, 250)

> For the time being, any elaboration of 'authentic' man must retreat into the background with respect to its precondition, namely the existence of a humanity within an accessible nature. With respect to the question, which remains open, that asks what man ought to be (a question that is subject to mutable answers), in light of the total threat that characterizes the present moment of universal history, we are taken back to the primary claim that has always underlaid that question, but has until now never become actual, that is the claim that commands that man himself ought to be, though still as a man.[3]

Analogously he says:

> Das Erste ist das Seinsollen des Objekts, das Zweite das Tunsollen des zur Sachwaltung berufenen Subjekts.
>
> (Jonas 1979, 175)

> The primary claim is the ought-to-be of the object, the secondary claim is the ought-to-do of the subject that is called to govern it.[4]

The preservation of the earth in order to assure the permanence of human life is assumed, not only as a desirable end but as an end in itself. Its actualization is introduced as an obligation necessary in itself, so that the assurance of the permanence of human life on earth is assumed as the reason on the grounds of which future ethics may be established in the first place. Jonas's conceptualization of responsibility is itself a response to the obligation indicated earlier in the text, in that it conceives responsibility as a means to fulfill the presupposed end, that is, the presupposed permanence of human life on earth. This is to say that by responding to the ecological imperative, the notion of responsibility is assumed in operative terms as a means to actualize this presupposed obligation. The ecological imperative, however, is not informed by a principle of perfection but by the mere demand to overcome an eminent menace that imperils the permanence of human life on earth. The assurance of this permanence becomes the source of meaning for responsible human practices, whereas the originating interrogative of classical ethics is relinquished on behalf of it. The reason on the grounds of which Jonas's imperative is established is informed by contingency inasmuch as, for example, an interrogating stance toward "human life" or "authenticity" is not required for its formulation. Quite the contrary! The likeliness of such an interrogating stance is subjected to the permanence of "human life", which is assumed as "factum brutum" without any further need for interrogation. The stance in which man responds to brute facts—to "lived impacts" in a contingent context—requires no true responsibility but rather mere responsiveness, that is, decisions that do not involve a judgment with regard to sense, but tend to evolve into a mere reaction to contingent beings, the sense of which is already predefined by their operability in the functional context within which the persistence of human life on earth is ascertained. Functionality then takes the place of the criterion of truth. What operates in a functional context appears to be true.

4.3 John Maurice Clark's Changing Basis of Economic Responsibility

As has been stated in the first part of this book,[5] according to validated historical reconstructions (cf. Haase 2017; Köhne 2017), the concept of economic responsibility, as we know it today, was first introduced by John Maurice Clark in an article entitled *The Changing Basis of Economic Responsibility*, published in 1916. It was his intent to overcome an "anachronism" (Clark 1916, 209) that consisted in the opinion that economic responsibility could be conceived as mere "responsibility of the individual for his own economic destiny: his responsibility for paying his debts and keeping out of the poor-house" (Clark 1916, 209). However, Clark states,

> the ideas of obligation which embody the actual relations of man to man [...], and answer the needs of the twentieth century, are radically different from the ideas which dominated [past centuries].
>
> (Clark 1916, 209)

As a consequence, "we have inherited an economics of irresponsibility" (1916, 209), unable to cope with present problems which have to be considered in the light of

> new ideas of cause and effect, [which require] new ideas of responsibility.
>
> (Clark 1916, 2013)

He anticipates the insight that the rise of concepts of responsibility to become key concepts of our time is the direct consequence of profound transformation processes taking place in various spheres of human practices. In the course of these processes—as a consequence of the ongoing transformation—a series of problems arose in view of which the conceptualization of economic responsibility appeared to be indicated, inasmuch as economic responsibility appeared to have a strong problem-solving and even problem-preventing potential. Accordingly, Clark states:

> We need all the sense of responsibility we can arouse, of all kinds, organized and directed in the most intelligent and efficient channels to make even moderate satisfactory headway with the increasingly complex problems that are piling up ahead of us.
>
> (Clark 1916, 217)

And he continues:

> We are coming to see that our everyday business dealings have more far-reaching effects than we have ever realized, and that the system of free contract is by itself quite inadequate to bring home the responsibility for these effects.
>
> (Clark 1916, 2018)

The manifold challenges implied by the aforementioned transformation process have led to a discussion of the notion of responsibility in light of the question of attribution, which recently has appeared as the core question referring to concepts of responsibility (c.f. Jonas 1979; Lenk 2017; Loth 2017). This has far-reaching implications for the understanding of responsibility, implications that define the scope of the conceptualization of economic responsibility to this day. The problem of attribution emerges on the grounds of the condition that responsibility is tied to a linear relationship between an acting subject and the effects of their action (c.f. De Gennaro, Lüfter 2018). The notion of economic responsibility is by implication defined by this linear relationship and thus confined to a restricted context of action within which pressing problems require effective responses. As long as these responses and their effects are justified by the pressing nature of eminent problems, the premise of reason introduced earlier seems to be suspended, when, in fact, it is not. It seems to be suspended due to the fact that the imperative of operability recommends and justifies the application of these concepts within a functional context. As was already shown, the emergence of problems as well as their urgency subsists exclusively on the grounds of a predefined functional context. However, the assumption itself of this predefined functional context remains unquestioned, whereas it would require a further questioning, namely, a reduction-to-reason, for the originating interrogative to be restored which allots and bestows the ethical dimension, that is, the dimension which allows for and welcomes human dwelling in the first place.

Consequently, the urgency of context-related problems does not provide evidence of the presence of true obligations which could be introduced as an answer to the guiding question of modern ethics, "What ought I to do?". The notion of economic responsibility cannot be reduced to its responsive character alone, however efficient it may seem, neither can true obligations be replaced by the operative urgency of context-dependent problems. This urgency subsists only on the grounds of a restricted functional context of action; it does not subsist by itself. Urgency refers to problems which emerge in a predefined functional context and require responsive actions on the condition that the said problems interfere with the persistence of the said context, though not unconditionally so. According to Kant, we can state that these problems inform obligations on a hypothetical rather than a categorical level, that is, obligations of a second order, not true obligations of the first order. This is to say that the original dimension, which allows for and welcomes human dwelling in the first place, is replaced, without giving any further reason, by a predefined functional context that is assumed randomly.

The discussion of the notion of economic responsibility, prevalent in light of the problem of attribution, meets today's understanding of the expression "to be responsible" which, according to the aforementioned definition of the *Oxford English Dictionary*, means "to be capable to fulfill an obligation". The attribution of economic responsibility on the basis of the notion of a linear relationship between an acting subject— be it a nation, an organization, a collective, or an individual—and the effects of their action is, on the one hand, determined by the ability to achieve an effect and, on the other hand, by the subsistence of a true obligation as ultimate reason. What we see, at this point, is that the notion of economic responsibility, based on the notion of a linear relationship between acting subjects and the effects of their action, is in itself insufficient to define the notion of responsibility as such, so that the scope of this linear relationship must include the notion of an end in the form of an effect that ought to be fulfilled by obligation. In the sense assumed here, "to be responsible" means, in the first place, "to be capable of responding to an obligation". In other words, the said obligation should appear to be an end that ought to be actualized through action, as an effect of that action. Consequently, it is this end that offers the ultimate reason for being responsible, as far as it is open to being actualized as a desirable effect. As this very reason it offers, secondly, an action-orientation insofar as it is open not only to being actualized, but ought to be actualized. Consequently, as this reason, it offers, thirdly, a decision-making criterion on the basis of which an action can be considered responsible or irresponsible, insofar as, exclusively thanks to said criterion, we can state that an obligation was fulfilled, or remained unfulfilled, or was fulfilled to some extent.

4.4 The Friedman Doctrine

What is now generally referred to as the "Friedman Doctrine" may serve as an example of this conceptualization of responsibility. In an article published in 1970 by the *New York Times Magazine*, titled *The Social Responsibility of Business Is to Increase Its Profits*, Milton Friedman sustains that it is not a given that we speak about something like business responsibilities, management responsibilities, economic responsibilities, as if there are major implications beyond the scope of business, beyond the scope of management, beyond the scope of economics, which can aspire to some ultimate status. His article directly addresses the scope of responsibility, as he argues that in the case of business as well as management and economics, responsibility is confined to a restricted context of action predefined by what is assumed to be business reason, management reason, or, generally speaking, economic reason.

> When I hear businessmen speak eloquently about the 'social responsibilities in a free-enterprise system', I am reminded of the wonderful line about the Frenchman who discovered at the age of 70 that he has been speaking prose all his life. The businessmen believe that they are defending free enterprise when they declaim that business is not concerned 'merely' with profit but also with promoting desirable 'social' ends. [...] In fact they are [...] preaching pure and unadulterated socialism. Businessmen who talk this way are unwitting puppets of the intellectual forces that have been undermining the basis of free society these past decades.
>
> (Friedman 1970)

By assuming unquestioningly that the notion of responsibility is defined by the notion of a linear relationship between the acting subject and the effects of their action, and thereby confined to a restricted context of action—the economic context—Friedman adopts the notion of profit as an ultimate end which ought to be pursued and eventually realized. This is to say that within the economic context, profit turns out to be a good reason to do one thing and to abstain from doing the other. It offers an action-orientation, insofar as it is open not only to being realized but ought to be realized in the first place, as long as a predefined economic context is accepted. Furthermore, it offers a decision-making criterion on the grounds of which actions can be considered to be economically responsible or economically irresponsible.

> There is one and only one social responsibility of business—to use its resources and engage in activities designed to increase its profits so long as it stays within the rules of the game, which is to say engages in open and free competition without deception and fraud.
>
> (Friedman 1970)

In a free-enterprise, private property system, a corporate executive is an employee of the owners of the business. He has direct responsibility to his employers. That responsibility is to conduct the business in accordance with their desires, which generally will be to make as much money as possible while conforming to the basic rules of the society, both those embodied in law and those embodied in ethical custom.[...] Of course, the corporate executive is also a person in his own right. As a person, he may have many other responsibilities that he recognizes or assumes voluntarily—to his family, his conscience, his feelings of charity, his church, his clubs, his city, his country. [...] If we wish, we may refer to some of these responsibilities as 'social responsibilities'. But in these respects he is acting as a principle, not an agent; he is spending his own money or time or energy, not the money of the employers or the time or energy he has contracted to devote to their purposes. If these are 'social responsibilities', they are the social responsibilities of individuals, not business.

(Friedman 1970)

Friedman is not denying that there may be some contexts of action beyond the economic one, where it seems to be reasonable that some other ends ought to be realized, so that what is considered to be responsible changes accordingly. Nonetheless, following his argumentation, the constellation between the notion of an end that ought to be realized through action, the notion of an action in terms of a linear relationship between acting subject and the effects of their actions, and the notion of a predefined action context does not change. And we see that, according to Friedman, different contexts always imply different ends. Different ends inform different contexts. We can therefore imagine that different contexts may exist simultaneously without interference, just as we might imagine the collision or even the superposition of different contexts. It does not change, in principle, the assumed constellation. This is to say that the problem raised earlier persists: namely, that the premise of the precedence of reason is not sufficiently settled as long as no end necessary in itself can be adduced. At the same time, the supposed constellation that bears the concept of responsibility follows this premise as long as it claims to be reasonable and not merely arbitrary. All context-dependent ends remain unreasonable, that is, constantly in need of a reduction-to-reason, just as all related obligations and responsibilities appear to be questionable. The problem of the insufficiency raised is a constitutive part of the concepts of responsibility presented here, and therefore one of its implicit traits which emerges against the backdrop of the tradition of metaphysical thinking, that is, against the backdrop of a classical position of ethics, such as that of Kant, and its accompanying fundamental questions. These questions may be said to be ethical insofar as they remain related to the whole of sense relations of human existence, that is, to the dimension which allows for and welcomes human dwelling in the first place. However, this dimension can be interrogated only within the wider interrogation of being.

The aforementioned constellation persists, regardless of whether we assume that by satisfying the Friedman Doctrine, businessmen contribute to the wealth of society in general, and therefore act in its best interests, or we assume just the opposite— that by satisfying the Friedman Doctrine, businessmen contribute to the decline of wealth of society in general, and therefore act against its best interests. Inevitably, the said questions of ethical character emerge, not least, in light of this constellation. As long as we are unable to reduce-to-reason the original dimension wherefrom the context of action, as well as its related end, was adduced, concepts of economic responsibility remain ungrounded. Ethical questions inform the conceptualization of economic responsibility, at least as long as the conceptualization is determined by the assumption that "to be responsible" means "to be capable of fulfilling an obligation", presupposing that "to fulfill" means "to act in the sense of producing effects", on the basis of a linear relationship between the acting subject and the effects of their action, within a predefined function.

4.5 Economic responsibility and truth

In conclusion, considering the emergence of ethical questions without pretermitting the precedence of the reason, a further distinction, introduced by Kant in his essay *What is enlightenment?*, will help us to discuss the scope of the concepts of economic responsibility: namely, the distinction drawn between the private and public use of reason.

According to the *Oxford English Dictionary*, one of the main meanings of the word "reason" is the "ability to adopt an action to a certain end". Actions that appear to be reasonably responsible are characterized by "the human ability to fulfill an obligation" (responsibility) by means of "adopting an action to an end" (reasonably on good grounds). This is to say that the distinction drawn between the private and public use of reason will be related to the human ability to realize an end through action. To be more precise, the said distinction will be related to the original human ability to be responsible in a way that is supposed to be reasonable.

> Faulheit und Feigheit sind die Ursachen, warum ein so großer Teil der Menschen, nachdem sie die Natur längst von fremder Leitung freigesprochen, dennoch gern zeitlebens unmündig bleiben; und warum es anderen so leicht wird, sich zu deren Vormündern aufzuwerfen. Es ist so bequem unmündig zu sein. Habe ich ein Buch, das für mich Verstand hat, einen Seelsorger der für mich Gewissen hat, einen Arzt, der für mich die Diät beurteilt usw., so brauche ich mich ja nicht selbst zu bemühen. Ich habe nicht nötig zu denken, wenn ich nur bezahlen kann.
>
> (Kant, WA, AA 08: A 482)

> Laziness and cowardice are the reasons why such a large part of mankind gladly remain minors all their lives, long after nature has freed them from external guidance. They are the reasons why it is so easy for others to set themselves up as guardians. It is so comfortable to be a minor. If I have a book that thinks for me, a pastor who acts as my conscience, a physician who prescribes my diet, and so on—then I have no need to exert myself. I have no need to think, if only I can pay.[6]

When Kant says "to exert myself" (i.e. to bother, to make an effort), he actually means "to be what I am" in the sense of "to be what I already am", that is, "to become what I already was".

> Zu dieser Aufklärung aber wird nichts erfordert als Freiheit; und zwar die unschädlichste unter allem, was nur Freiheit heißen mag, nämlich die: von seiner Vernunft in allen Stücken öffentlichen Gebrauch zu machen. Nun höre ich aber von allen Seiten rufen: Räsoniert nicht! Der Offizier sagt: Räsoniert nicht, sondern exerziert! Der Finanzrat: Räsoniert nicht, sondern bezahlt! Der Geistliche: Räsoniert nicht, sondern glaubt! Nur ein einziger Herr in der Welt sagt: Räsoniert, soviel ihr wollt, aber gehorcht! [...] Der öffentliche Gebrauch seiner Vernunft muß jederzeit frei sein, und der allein kann Aufklärung unter Menschen zustande bringen.
>
> (Kant, WA, AA 08: A 484)

> Enlightenment requires nothing but freedom—and the most innocent of all that may be called 'freedom': freedom to make public use of one's reason in all matters. Now I hear the cry from all

sides: "Do not reason!" The officer says: "Do not reason—drill!" The tax collector: "Do not reason—pay!" The pastor: "Do not reason—believe!" Only one ruler in the world says: "Reason as much as you please, but obey!" [...] The public use of one's reason must be free at all times, and this alone can bring enlightenment to mankind.[7]

The ruler here, we should like to assume, is truth. Here and now, we certainly cannot carry out a thorough study of the nature of truth, either in the sense in which the metaphysical tradition developed it or in the precise sense in which Kant understood it. But we can introduce truth as the assumed end of the public use of reason. This is to say that truth implies something like a human togetherness, a human coalescence, insofar as it indicates that dimension on which we, as human beings, ultimately rely (cf. Borghi 2011). Consequently, according to Kant, truth is the dimension of reliance that allows for human togetherness, human coalescence. We may add that, in this regard, ἦθος is the Greek name of this dimension.

Something turns out to be true, inasmuch as human beings rely on it in the first place, when relating to what is [not human?], when relating to other human beings, when relating to themselves.

> The trait of reliance is confirmed by the way in which the English language itself understands the word 'truth' (that stems from an Old-English word that means 'faithful, trust, trustworthy'). For instance, what we call 'a true argument' is not primarily an argument which is factually or rationally correct, but an argument we can rely on. Similarly, a 'true hammer' is not just a hammer which is non-imaginary and 'real' but primarily a hammer we can trustfully rely on when hammering a nail to the wall [...] A 'true man' is someone on whose humanity we can rely.
>
> (Borghi 2011, 16 f.)

Any form of human togetherness, any form of human coalescence remains from the ground up tied to the notion of truth. Therefore, the end of the public use of reason is, according to Kant, the furtherance and the maintenance, and eventually the realization of truth as reliance. The claim for the realization of the said end is a true obligation, which can be fulfilled exclusively by men who can afford freedom, that is, by human beings who have the courage to make public use of their own reason in all matters and who, therefore, are able to act in a responsible way.

Ich verstehe aber unter dem öffentlichen Gebrauch seiner Vernunft denjenigen, den jemand als Gelehrter vor dem ganzen Publikum der Leserwelt macht. Den Privatgebrauch nenne ich denjenigen, den er in einem gewissen ihm anvertrauten bürgerlichen Posten oder Amte von seiner Vernunft machen darf. Nun ist zu manchen Geschäften, die in das Interesse des gemeinen Wesens laufen, ein gewisser Mechanismus notwendig, vermittelst dessen einige Glieder des gemeinsamen Wesens sich bloß passiv verhalten müssen, um durch eine künstliche Einhelligkeit von der Regierung zu öffentlichen Zwecken gerichtet oder wenigstens von der Zerstörung dieser Zwecke abgehalten zu werden. Hier ist es nun freilich nicht erlaubt zu räsonnieren, sondern man muss gehorchen [...] So würde es sehr verderblich sein, wenn ein Offizier, dem von seinen Oberen etwas anbefohlen wird, im Dienste über die Zweckmäßigkeit oder Nützlichkeit dieses Befehls laut vernünfteln wollte; er muss gehorchen. Es kann ihm aber billigermaßen nicht verwehrt werden, als Gelehrter über die Fehler im Kriegsdienst Anmerkungen zu machen und diesem seinem Publikum zur Beurteilung vorzulegen. [...] [A]ls Gelehrter, der durch die Schriften zum eigentlichen Publikum redet, nämlich der Welt spricht, [...] genießt einer uneingeschränkte Freiheit, sich seiner eigenen Vernunft zu bedienen und in seiner eigenen Person zu sprechen.

(Kant, WA, AA 08: 485–488)

By 'public use of one's reason' I mean that use which a man, as scholar, makes of it before the reading public. I call 'private use' that use which a man makes of his reason in a civic post that has been entrusted to him. In some affairs affecting the interest of the community a certain mechanism is necessary in which some members of the community remain passive. This creates an artificial unanimity which will serve the fulfillment of public objectives, or at least keep these objectives from being destroyed. Here reasoning is not permitted: one must obey. Thus it would be very unfortunate if an officer on duty and under orders from his superiors should want to criticize the appropriateness or utility of his orders. He must obey. But as a scholar he could not rightfully be prevented from taking notice of the mistakes in the military service and from submitting his views to his public for its judgment. [...] [A]s the scholar who speaks to his own public (the world) through his writings, [...] enjoys unlimited freedom to use its own reason and to speak for himself.[8]

If the concept of economic responsibility is supposed to sustain the claim that human beings "ought to" act for good reasons, then, in

Kant's view, this occurs only if human beings make public use of their reason—that is, of their ability to fulfill an obligation by adopting an action to the said end, in other words, the obligation to enlighten all aspects of the dimension on which they, as human beings, rely in the first place. As long as human beings make only private use of their reason, they do not act responsibly but only for reasons of mere context-dependent ends, which cannot be considered to maintain, further, and eventually realize reliance as such.

In order to add one more degree of precision, we may say that the intended end must be understood according to the German word "öffentlich". In fact, the English word "public" is not fit for translating "öffentlich" in the sense in which Kant understands it. The meaning of "öffentlich" goes in the direction of what is "open", in the sense of "open to question", and thus requires in and of itself to be pondered, to be thought about, and that which therefore remains the constant source of any genuine human reasoning. What is "open" in this way is—ultimately and ever again—the question of being. Now it seems quite clear why the private use of reason is irresponsible. It is, from the start, subjected to the presupposed end of a predefined context which is never "open", never "open to questions". What emerges is not reliable inasmuch as the assumed context and the assumed end are not seen in their questionability, but rather adopted as a given. Thus, no reduction-to-reason, no bearing of the openness of being itself can take place. The human togetherness can be thought of as a coalescence, where human beings are bound by the circumstance that they share a responsibility toward truth itself. Everyone is expected to contribute—and one does so by simply having the courage to make "public", "openness-bearing" use of one's capability to adopt one's thinking and acting to an end that must be, every time anew said.

Notes

1 Trans. by Ivo De Gennaro.
2 Trans. by Ivo De Gennaro.
3 Trans. by Ivo De Gennaro.
4 Trans. by Ivo De Gennaro.
5 See above, p. 1.
6 Trans. by Paul Guyer and Allen W. Wood (Kant 2003).
7 Trans. by Paul Guyer and Allen W. Wood (Kant 2003).
8 Trans. by Paul Guyer and Allen W. Wood (Kant 2003).

5   Outlook

The two kinds of responsibility discussed in the context of the present research—operability-based responsibility and end-in-itself-based responsibility—are related, even though in fundamentally different ways, to the assumption of an obligation that ought to be fulfilled through human practice. In line with this correlation, the standard definition of "responsibility" introduced earlier considers human practices to be responsible when they demonstrate their "capability to fulfil an obligation". Accordingly, within the tradition of modern metaphysical ethics, the assumption of an obligation reveals itself as the reason on the ground of which the conceptualization of responsibility occurs. This is to say that the character of the obligation decides which kind of responsibility will come into view. As a consequence, economic responsibility is conceived on the basis of the assumption of an economic obligation that defines the scope of the related responsibility, and thus constrains it to the functional contexts which, in turn, are assumed to have an "economic" character.

Our analysis has shown, on the one hand, that the conceptualization of responsibility remains with "one foot in the air" (Kant, KrV A 467 / B 495) as long as the obligation is merely presupposed but not sufficiently interrogated with regard to its origin. On the other hand, it has shown that this origin announces itself in the claiming need for a sufficient response to an interrogative, which is not based *a priori* on the assumption of an obligation but is related to man's understanding of being. This understanding is neither a general competence nor an individual talent, but the native trait of man's own being which allows each one of us to become the unique and incomparable being he or she already is. At the same time, the understanding of being is the pivot of the human togetherness, when the latter is not merely conceived as the means for the actualization of shared objectives but as an instance of true coalescence.

The strengthening and preservation of this trait of coalescence is the genuine responsibility of any form of human knowledge, thus also for economics. The relation of the aforementioned interrogative to man's understanding of being emerges through the question of being, which could provide a starting point for future research in the field. All the more so as precisely this question turns out to be the latent ground of the occidental tradition of thinking. Because this ground has remained latent, the claiming need for a response to the interrogative which emerges through that question has been neglected up to our days (cf. Heidegger 1993). As a consequence, the awareness for this interrogative implies a widening of the scope of the notion of economic responsibility; in fact, responsibility itself could in the first place be conceived as an element for a new determination of economic knowledge that goes beyond the scope of economics as a modern, methodical science. Economics itself emerges as a form of knowledge which offers a response to the interrogative while building, in the first place, on man's understanding of being. This is to say that the understanding of being bears this interrogative as its origin, while all forms of knowledge which build on this understanding emerge in light of the interrogative itself. On this basis, a third notion of responsibility becomes likely. This notion namely emerges in light of the understanding of being, where the latter is not conceived offhand in terms of an obligation—neither in the sense of an operative obligation nor in the sense of an obligation necessary in itself—but as containing within itself the claiming need for a response that requires to be borne in and through man's own being.

With regard to this conjunction, it could be conducive to future research perspectives to examine how, within the tradition of modern metaphysical ethics, man's understanding of being is conceived as the ability of man (i.e. the subject) to maintain a relation to beings (i.e. objects) by knowing them in what they are in the first place. The meant ability is traced back to the transcendent character of man, namely, to the fact that while man finds himself exposed to beings, he also finds himself having had to transcend (to go beyond, to exceed) them toward the constitutive trait of their being (i.e. their beingness) in order to achieve adequate knowledge about them. Throughout modernity, beginning with Descartes, the reason on the ground of which this ability is established, and thus the truth of man's understanding of being is ascertained, is found in man himself. It is neither seen in the ἀλήθεια of φύσις, which constituted the fundamental understanding of being in Greek thinking nor in the revealed truth of the Almighty God as the creator of all beings. In other words, the response to the aforementioned interrogative is found in man himself being his own ground and thereby being the ground of beings as such and in whole. "This circumstance is indicated in the word that, alone, names the fundamental trait of modern philosophy, namely, subjectivity (from the Latin sub-iectum = what is thrown, and thus lies under: the underlying)" (De Gennaro 2019, 233). This is to say that if within modern metaphysical ethics, the conceptualization of responsibility originates from and, in a sense, as a response to the aforementioned interrogative, the latter is from the outset constrained by subjectivism and as a consequence neglected as such. In fact, the response to the meant interrogative is anticipated by man's subjectivity as the exclusive determinant, viz. as the principle of being. What would it mean to suspend this determinant? What are the implications of this suspension? What would it mean to think in the occurrence of this suspension? What is required from thinking within this occurrence? Are we already prepared to think the suspension in the occurrence of the suspension itself? What will then sustain the truth of man's understanding of being?

The suspension of subjectivism, however, inaugurates a yet untrodden path of interrogation regarding the notion of responsibility. This path is precisely what is tentatively intended by the formula "being-related responsibility", introduced earlier. Formally speaking, the originating interrogative, which emerges through the question of being, emerges as an instant of reaffirming man's understanding of being within the suspension of subjectivism and thus to renew the foundation of his abode in the midst of beings in the whole, that is, to renew the foundation of the dimension named in the Greek word ἦθος. The renewal of the question of ethics does not occur for the mere sake of renewal, but as an attempt to respond to the yet neglected interrogative and thus as an attempt to think the interrogative itself as an instant for the foundation of ethics. This is to say that the renewal of the question of ethics is bound to man's understanding of being, which, within the occidental tradition of thinking, springs as distinct experience of man's freedom to say being. This is to say that it springs as distinct experience of the withdrawal of being which emerges in the question of being as originating interrogative and which requires man's freedom from any metaphysical determinant. In other words, the question of ethics is in and of itself related to the question of being, while the question of being is in and of itself related to the question of ethics. In light of subjectivism, the two questions refer to different objects of knowledge, and thus they appear as separate questions. On the other hand, in light of the suspension of subjectivism, this separation no longer applies, so that the relation of the two questions has to be rethought, and the attempt to bring the ethical dimension of responsibility to light is intrinsically related to man's understanding of being, that is, to the necessity to say being.

Man's understanding of being—thought of in the suspension of subjectivism—refers, in and of itself, to a distinct responsibility. It is neither the responsibility of a subject nor the responsibility for an object. The meant responsibility is at the origin of the subject-object relation, but it never presupposes this relation, and thus it is not the expression of what occurs between a subject and its objects. It is not based on any evident obligation or on any presupposed obligation inasmuch as it is not based on any evidence or presupposition whatsoever. This is to say that the meant responsibility relieves itself from the involvement with contingency. Its semblances vaguely appear as we begin to see that the expression "man's understanding of being" does not indicate the "capability to understand" of a contingent "man" that is situated in a contingent "there", but indicates the existence of man himself, that is, man's being.[1] According to the literal sense of "responsibility", man's understanding of being refers to the "renewal of the promise to be" required by the aforementioned interrogative through which the openness of the yet unthought question of being appears. Within this, openness beings are liberated in their promise to be. Thus, man's understanding of being is responsible inasmuch as it is, in and of itself, the "renewed pledge" on this openness, that is, the "renewed pledge" on the promise to be. In other words, man's understanding of being is responsible inasmuch as it is, in and of itself, the awareness of the openness that appears through the claiming need for a human abiding by the promise to be.

No doubt these are only tentative allusions to what could matter to a future research on the notion of economic responsibility. The very formula "being-related responsibility" is no more than a first hint in the direction of a field of study that, to this day, lies idle.

Note

1 In this context, Heidegger's *Dasein* is of particular interest. In fact, *Dasein* could become the ground-word of the attempt to think the notion of responsibility in the sense of what here is tentatively indicated as being-related responsibility.

Bibliography

Abend, Gabriel (2013). The Origin of Business Ethics in American Universities. 1902–1936, in: *Business Ethics Quarterly* 23(2), pp. 171–205.

Alemann, Anette von (2015). *Gesellschaftliche Verantwortung und ökonomische Handlungslogik. Deutungsmuster von Führungskräften der deutschen Wirtschaft*, Springer VS: Wiesbaden.

Aras, Güler / Growrher, David (2010). *A Handbook of Corporate Governance and Social Responsibility*, Routledge: London.

Balluchi, Federica / Furlotti, Katia [ed.] (2017). *La responsabilità sociale delle imprese. Un percorso verso lo sviluppo sostenibile. Profili di governance e di accountability*, G. Giappichelli Editore: Torino.

Bayertz, Kurt (1995). Eine kurze Geschichte der Herkunft der Verantwortung, in: Kurt Bayertz (ed.), *Verantwortung. Prinzip oder Problem?* WBG: Darmstadt, pp. 3–71.

Bayertz, Kurt / Beck, Birgit (2017). Der Begriff der Verantwortung in der Moderne: 19.-20. Jahrhundert, in: Ludger Heidbrink, Claus Langbehn, Janina Loh (eds.), *Handbuch Verantwortung*, Springer: Berlin, pp. 133–148.

Bazargan-Forward, Saba / Tollefsen, Deborah [ed.] (2020). *The Routledge Handbook of Collective Responsibility*, Routledge: London.

Borghi, Maurizio (2011). Copyright and Truth, in: *Theoretical Inquiries in Law* 12(1), pp. 1–27.

Carroll, Archie B. (1979). A Three-Dimensional Model of Corporate Performance, in: *Academy of Management Review* 4(4), pp. 497–505.

Carroll, Archie B. (1991). The Pyramid of Corporate Social Responsibility. Toward the Moral Management of Organizational Stakeholders, in: *Business Horizons* 34(4), pp. 39–48.

Clark, John Maurice (1915). The Concept of Value, in: *The Quarterly Journal of Economics* 29, pp. 663–673.

Clark, John Maurice (1916). The Changing Basis of Economic Responsibility, in: *Journal of Political Economy* 24(1–2), pp. 209–229.

Davila, Ana Maria (2016). *Human Dignity and Managerial Responsibility*, Routledge: London.

58   *Bibliography*

De Gennaro, Ivo (2006). Building Leadership on the Invaluable. Towards the Groundworks for a Phenomenological Approach to the Philosophy of Management, in: *Ancilla Iuris* 78, pp. 78–87.

De Gennaro, Ivo / Zaccaria, Gino (2011). *La dittatura del valore. L'insegnamento e la ricerca nell'università planetaria: The dictatorship of value. Teaching and research in the planetary university*, Mac-Graw-Hill: Milano.

De Gennaro, Ivo (2013). *The Weirdness of Being. Heidegger's Unheard Answer to the Seinsfrage.* Acumen: Durham.

De Gennaro, Ivo / Kazmierski, Sergiusz / Lüfter, Ralf / Simon, Robert [ed.] (2013 f.). *Wirtliche Ökonomie. Philosophische und dichterische Quellen*, Traugott Bautz: Nordhausen.

De Gennaro, Ivo / Lüfter, Ralf (2018). La perfezione tra passato e futuro. Per una diagnosi etica della responsabilità sociale, in: Franco Miano (ed.), *Etica e responsabilità*, Orthotes: Napoli-Salerno, pp. 145–156.

De Gennaro, Ivo (2019). *Principles of Philosophy. A Phenomenological Approach*, Alber: Freiburg.

Delbeck, Petra (2008). *Ethikbasierte Investmentfonds. Ein Performancevergleich mit traditionellen Investmentfonds*, Druck Diplomica: Hamburg.

Fonnesu, Luca (2017). Der Begriff der Verantwortung in der Neuzeit und in der Aufklärung, in: Ludger Heidbrink, Claus Langbehn, Janina Loh (eds.), *Handbuch Verantwortung,* Springer: Berlin, pp. 111–132.

Friedman, Milton (1970). The Social Responsibility of Business Is to Increase Its Profits, in: *New York Times Magazine* (13.09.1970).

Gedinat, Jürgen (2015). *Ein Modell von Welt. Unterwegs in der Globalisierung*, Centaurus Verlag: Herbolzheim.

Haase, Michaela (2017). The Changing Basis of Economic Responsibility. Zur Bedeutung und Rezeption von John Maurice Clarks Artikel zur ökonomischen Verantwortung, in: Diskussionsbeiträge. Fachbereich Wirtschaftswissenschaft. Freie Universität Berlin, https://papers.ssrn.com/sol3/papers. cfm?abstract_id=2997105 (14.01.2019).

Hasnas, John (2012). Reflections on Corporate Moral Responsibility and the Problem Solving Technique of Alexander the Great, in: *Journal of Business Ethics* 107(2), pp. 183–195.

Heidbrink, Ludger / Hirsch, Alfred [ed.] (2008). *Verantwortung als marktwirtschaftliches Prinzip*, Campus Verlag: Frankfurt & New York.

Heidbrink, Ludger (2017). Definitionen und Voraussetzungen der Verantwortung, in: Ludger Heidbrink, Claus Langbehn, Janina Loh (eds.), *Handbuch Verantwortung*, Springer: Berlin, pp. 3–34.

Heidegger, Martin (1993). *Sein und Zeit*, Max Niemeyer Verlag: Tübingen.

Heidegger, Martin (1994). *Heraklit, HGA 55*, Vittorio Klostermann: Frankfurt am Main.

Heidegger, Martin (1994[a]). *Vom Wesen der menschlichen Freiheit, HGA 31*, Vittorio Klostermann: Frankfurt am Main.

Heidegger, Martin (1997). *Was heißt Denken?* Max Niemeyer Verlag: Tübingen.

Heidegger, Martin (1998). *Nietzsche*, Neske: Stuttgart.

Heidegger, Martin (1998ᵃ). *Einführung in die Metaphysik*, Max Niemeyer Verlag: Tübingen.

Heidegger, Martin (1998ᵇ). *Kant und das Problem der Metaphysik*, Vittorio Klostermann: Frankfurt am Main.

Heidegger, Martin (1999). *The Principle of Reason*, trans. by Reginald Lilly, Indiana University Press: Bloomington & Indianapolis.

Heidegger, Martin (2000). *Über den Humanismus*, Vittorio Klostermann: Frankfurt am Main.

Heidegger, Martin (2000ᵃ). *Introduction to Metaphysics*, trans. by Gregory Fried and Richard Polt, Yale University Press: New Haven & London.

Heidegger, Martin (2006). *Der Satz vom Grund*, Klett-Cotta: Stuttgart.

Heidegger, Martin (2007). *Was ist Metaphysik?* Vittorio Klostermann: Frankfurt am Main.

Heidegger, Martin (2008). *Identität und Differenz*, Klett-Cotta: Stuttgart.

Heidegger, Martin (2009). *What Is Called Thinking?* trans. by Gelnn Gray, Harper Perennial: New York.

Hölderlin, Friedrich (1966). *Poems and Fragments*, trans. by Miachael Hamburger, Routledge: London.

Jonas, Hans (1979). *Das Prinzip Verantwortung. Versuch einer Ethik für die technologische Zivilisation*, Insel Verlag: Frankfurt am Main.

Kant, Immanuel (1998). *Critique of Pure Reason*, trans. by Paul Guyer and Allen W. Wood, Cambridge University Press: Cambridge.

Kant, Immanuel (2003). *The Cambridge Edition of the Works of Immanuel Kant*, trans. by Paul Guyer and Allen W. Wood, Cambridge University Press: Cambridge.

Kant, Immanuel (2011). *Werke in sechs Bänden*, WBG: Darmstadt.

Köhne, Ralf (2017). Ökonomische Verantwortung, in: Ludger Heidbrink, Claus Langbehn, Janina Loh (eds.), *Handbuch Verantwortung*, Springer: Berlin, pp. 607–621.

Lenk, Hans (2017). Verantwortlichkeit und Verantwortungstypen. Arten und Polaritäten, in: Ludger Heidbrink, Claus Langbehn, Janina Loh (eds.), *Handbuch Verantwortung*, Springer: Berlin, pp. 57–84.

Liddell, Henry George / Scott, Robert (1996). *Greek-English Lexicon*, Calderon Press: Oxford.

Loh, Janina (2017). Strukturen und Relata der Verantwortung, in: Ludger Heidbrink, Claus Langbehn, Janina Loh (eds.), *Handbuch Verantwortung*, Springer: Berlin, pp. 35–56.

Lüfter, Ralf (2015). The Future of Sustainability, in: *Philosophy Study* 3(5), pp. 155–161.

Lüfter, Ralf (2019). Ethical Implications of Economic Responsibilies, in: *Philosophy Study* 9(2), pp. 101–115.

Miano, Francesco [ed.] (2018). *Etica e Responsabilità*, Orthotes Editrice: Napoli & Salerno.

Miller, Seumas (2006). Collective Moral Responsibility: An Individualist Account, in: *Midwest Studies in Philosophy* 30(1), pp. 176–193.

Müller-Christ, Georg (2014). *Nachhaltiges Management. Einführung in Ressourcenorientierung und widersprüchliche Managementrationalität*, Nomos: Baden-Baden.

Nietzsche, Friedrich (1999). *Kritische Studienausgabe*, hrsg. von Giorgio Colli und Mazzino Montinari, Deutscher Taschenbuch Verlag: München.

Nilikant, Vekataraman (2012). *Managing Responsibility. Alternative Approaches to Corporate Managment and Governance*, Routledge: London.

Oxford English Dictionary [online]. https://www-oed-com.libproxy.unibz.it, accessed 6 March 2020 <https://www-oed-com.>

Rauen, Verena (2017). Ethische Verantwortung, in: Ludger Heidbrink, Claus Langbehn, Janina Loh (eds.), *Handbuch Verantwortung*, Springer: Berlin, pp. 545–558.

Sauvé Meyer, Susan / Hause, Jeffrey P. (2017). Der Begriff der Verantwortung in Antike und Mittelalter, in: Ludger Heidbrink, Claus Langbehn, Janina Loh (eds.), *Handbuch Verantwortung*, Springer: Berlin, pp. 87–109.

Velasquez, Manuel (2003). Debunking Corporate Moral Responsibility, in: *Business Ethics Quarterly* 13(4), pp. 531–562.

Vogel, David (2005). *The Market for Virtue: The Potential and Limits of Corporate Social Responsibility*, Brookings Institution Press: Washington.

Vogel, David (2010). The Private Regulation of Global Corporate Conduct: Achievements and Limitations, in: *Business & Society* 49(1), pp. 68–87.

Zaccaria, Gino (2017). Le questioni fondamentali della filosofia I, accessed 7 February 2020 <http://www.scienzanuova.org/it/>.

Zaccaria, Gino (2017ª). Tempo spazio arte, accessed 21 March 2020 <http://www.scienzanuova.org/it/>.

Zaccaria, Gino (2018). The Light of Cézanne (Errancy into the sun), eudia. Yearbook for Philosophy, Poetry, and Art (12/2018), accessed 7 February 2020 <http://www.eudia.org>.

Zaccaria, Gino (2019). *L'inizio greco del pensiero. Heidegger e l'essenza futura della filosofia*, Marinotti: Milano.

Index

Printed in the United States
by Baker & Taylor Publisher Services